LETHAL
LOVERS AND
POISONOUS
PEOPLE

LETHAL LOVERS AND POISONOUS PEOPLE

*How to Protect
Your Health
from Relationships
That Make You Sick*

Harriet B. Braiker, Ph.D.

POCKET BOOKS

New York   London   Toronto   Sydney   Tokyo   Singapore

POCKET BOOKS, a division of Simon & Schuster Inc.
1230 Avenue of the Americas, New York, NY 10020

Braiker, Dr. Harriet B., 1948–
    Lethal lovers and poisonous people : how to protect your health
from relationships that make you sick / Harriet B. Braiker.
      p. cm.
    Includes bibliographical references.
    ISBN: 0-671-72422-3 : $21.00
    1. Relationship addiction.   2. Interpersonal relations—Health
aspects.   3. Medicine, Psychosomatic.   I. Title.
RC552.R44B73   1992
158'.2—dc20   91-45558
                                         CIP

First Pocket Books hardcover printing June 1992

10 9 8 7 6 5 4 3 2 1

POCKET and colophon are registered trademarks of
Simon & Schuster Inc.

Printed in the U.S.A.

To Amanda,
for sharing her Mommy with this book and for teaching me about
a wondrous new kind of love

And to Amanda's Daddy,
who gave me a man to believe in

Contents

PART TWO

The Solution

Foreword

My purpose in writing *Lethal Lovers and Poisonous People: How to Protect Your Health from Relationships That Make You Sick* is to show you how significant relationships in your life can, over time, cause you severe physical and psychological damage.

Our health-conscious society has a collective obsession with finding ways to prolong life and ward off disease. To this end, we have become highly informed and responsible about the risks of smoking, high cholesterol, obesity, inadequate exercise, unsafe sex and other perilous health habits. In addition, we are increasingly vigilant to the hazards of invisible viruses and chemical toxins that threaten the safety of both our public environments and private homes.

But, for the most part, we have remained ignorant of an equal or even greater threat to our physical well-being: psychological poisons produced by toxic relationships, which can sabotage your body's ability to protect itself from illness and can cause serious and even fatal harm. As the medical research field of psychoneuroimmunology is revealing, our attitudes, emotions, moods, beliefs, and behavior play a key role in the function or dysfunction of our bodies. In our homes, workplaces, and personal environments, our negative reactions to other people can predispose us to ill health.

This book will help you develop a new awareness of the insidious and far-reaching effects that interpersonal problems can have on your susceptibility to illness. You will discover that phrases that you previously accepted as benign figures of speech contain far more than a grain of truth. The next time you hear yourself, or someone close to you, say, "He's breaking my heart," "My boss is giving me ulcers," "She's driving me crazy," or, "This relationship is killing me," you may in fact be hearing a dire prediction of a disturbing reality. As you will see, it is not a far leap from an aching heart to a heart attack.

The ways in which psychological poisons can wreak havoc on your health are illustrated throughout this book by actual case studies from my practice as a clinical psychologist. The cases represent only a small sample of the people I have treated who suffer from the effects of toxic relationships. Naturally, the names and identifying details of the individuals involved have been altered to protect their confidentiality. I am immeasurably grateful to my patients for trusting me with their intimate stories and for allowing me to help them detoxify their relationships and, in so doing, regain their health.

But negative emotions alone are rarely the *sole* cause of physical illness. Moreover, the guilt you inevitably will produce by erroneously assuming blame for "making" yourself sick will only compound your problems. Still, since toxic relationships *are* potent factors in undermining your health, my main purpose is to provide hope and guidance by giving you antidotes to the psychological poisons they produce. My detoxification techniques are those that I have used clinically with great success treating people in toxic relationships.

I don't wish to suggest that the methods offered in this book are substitutes for professional psychotherapy. On the contrary, should you have both the means and the motivation for therapy, my advice is to seek the help of a qualified mental health practitioner. The methods detailed here for detoxifying your relationship will serve as a valuable adjunct to your treatment.

However, if you are suffering in an unhappy relationship, you still need to know what to do *on your own* to help yourself. The consequence of doing nothing about your unhappiness is that you *will* wind up in the company of a professional sooner or later. But the professional will likely be a medical doctor, treating you for the illnesses that your negative emotions help to produce.

Lethal Lovers and Poisonous People: How to Protect Your Health from Relationships That Make You Sick is designed specifically to help you identify the types of relationship problems you have, to illustrate the possible consequences, and—most important—to guide you step by step through time-tested detoxification techniques.

This book will change your thinking about the risks to your health that result from allowing dangerous negative emotions to continue in your relationships. But my intention here is also to alert you to the good news: Healthy relationships create positive emotions that operate to protect your health and help you to recover from illness. The intimate bonds you have with other people that breed healing feelings—love, trust, hope, optimism, the will to live, faith, purpose, determination, laughter, and festivity—will help prolong your life and greatly enhance its quality.

So, if you discover that you have a lethal lover or find yourself involved in another kind of toxic relationship, take heart: That recognition and the remedies offered here could save your life.

PART ONE

The Problem

1

**Warning: This Relationship May Be
Harmful to Your Health**

For the third time in ten years of marriage, Linda has the sickening feeling that her husband, Peter, is cheating on her. Until this morning, she couldn't say exactly why she felt so suspicious other than simply "woman's intuition." Perhaps it was a slight but nevertheless perceptible change in his physical carriage—more self-confident, even preening. Maybe it was his recent pattern of uncharacteristic late meetings at the office that had aroused her discomfort. Or it might even have been his seeming renewed interest in having sex with her, which, in retrospect, appears to have been a coverup for his infidelity and an antidote for his guilt.

Now, as she carefully replaces this month's American Express bill in the top drawer of Peter's desk, the sickening feeling transforms into rage. The proof is all there: local hotel charges and restaurant bills on the very nights that he pretended to work late. As always, Peter has left a clearly marked paper trail.

As tears well up in her eyes, Linda's emotions run the gamut from self-blame (she had gained weight recently and felt less attractive) to anger, from depression to rage. "Men are such bastards," she mutters. And then, plaintively, "But what can I do?"

Briefly, she considers confronting Peter with his betrayal, then rejects the idea on the grounds that bringing the problem into the open will only make the relationship more uncomfortable and undermine the security of her two young children. Linda cannot imagine divorcing Peter. She still loves him, despite her hurt and anger. Besides, her strict Catholic upbringing makes divorce simply out of the question. So, she resolves to "wait it out" until Peter tires of his new girlfriend, as he did the other two times. Although her decision makes her feel helpless and deeply depressed, she reasons—or rationalizes—that she has no other option. She convinces herself that she must swallow her hurt and anger in order to save her marriage and protect her children.

As Linda sighs in sad resignation, she checks her watch. This morning she has an appointment with her doctor to perform some diagnostic tests on her stomach. At 40, Linda has not enjoyed good health. This year alone, she has visited her family physician more than ten times for recurrent bouts of flu, colds, and other viral infections. Now she has worrisome symptoms that indicate that she might have something more serious.

Linda wonders why her resistance to "bugs" is so poor. After all, as she tells her doctor, she gets ample sleep, takes vitamins daily, exercises fairly routinely, and leads what she perceives to be a reasonably healthy lifestyle. The doctor, who is also her personal friend, doesn't probe about possible problems in her marriage.

But Linda's marital problems have a lot to do with her susceptibility to viruses and her vulnerability to something even as serious as cancer.

Linda's husband is a Lethal Lover. And Linda's ways of reacting to Peter's infidelities—her suppressed anger, sense of futility, helplessness, and depression—are dangerous harbingers of illness. In short, Linda's relationship—or, more precisely, her response to it—is harmful to her health.

Dan, age 52, pays a dear price for his six-figure salary and the material comforts of his life. With no college degree, Dan counts himself among the very fortunate few who, by dint of sheer "stick-to-itiveness," personal loyalty, and an incredibly long fuse to his temper, have managed to advance to a career position of considerable status.

Dan is the executive vice president of a company whose founder, Hank, is an entirely self-made man with a terrific knack for business. The company owns and operates a chain of small, neighborhood convenience stores that has grown in twenty-five years from a single Mom-and-Pop operation to a multimillion-dollar business. But to Dan, Hank's business genius is overshadowed by his exceedingly difficult personality. Despite his financial success, Hank seems totally to lack common sense when it comes to separating his business from his personal and family problems.

Dan functions as Hank's right-hand man and confidant in a role that far exceeds the boundaries of anything that could be construed as business. Hank's six grown children (from his three failed marriages) are all employed by the company in one capacity or another—from secretary to controller—despite their lack of qualifications and abilities. In addition, Hank's kids have very serious personality problems: The eldest two sons are chronic drug and alcohol abusers; the youngest daughter has been caught embezzling funds from the business and stealing cash from her father; still another son is gay but depressed and confused about his sexual orientation; and four of the heirs apparent (including the addicts) have stormy, tenuous marriages. Hank's offspring are a handful and Dan's hands are the ones that are constantly filled. He regularly receives midnight phone calls from Hank directing him to obtain bail for a son who has been arrested, to mediate a daughter's marital dispute, or to chauffeur another offspring who is too inebriated to drive. To further complicate matters, Dan handles all communication and spousal support payments for two of his boss's former wives. In short, Dan is up to his ears in Hank's personal problems.

Hank has an explosive personality and volatile temper that Dan has passively tolerated for years. Dan allows himself to serve as the object of Hank's hostility and frustration. Behind his back, other members of management characterize Dan as a "high-priced whipping boy."

Frequently, Hank tears into Dan about some matter of minor, if not negligible, importance, lambasting him with personal insults and attacks on his intelligence and competence. Dan tries to convince himself that Hank's tirades are unfounded and his personal affronts unwarranted. Nevertheless, after each of Hank's outbursts, Dan's self-esteem takes a nosedive and he is depressed for several days. When Dan's self-esteem plummets, he turns to alcohol to anesthetize the pain. So, Dan has become a very heavy drinker, maybe even an alcoholic.

Dan's time is not his own; he is on call twenty-four hours a day, including weekends. Hank calls Dan numerous times each day, at all hours, with every kind of problem ranging from minor business questions ("Where did we put last year's tax returns?") to family crises ("Bob is missing again. His wife thinks he's out drinking and using cocaine and I want you to find him").

In recent months, Hank's family problems have increased, while his ability to cope with them has diminished. Consequently, Dan's headaches have grown—literally and figuratively. Dan never knows what Hank's mood will be or when Hank might order him to report to the office for an emergency meeting. A summons might come in the middle of the night; it could come at midafternoon on Sunday; or it might intrude on a Saturday evening when Dan and his wife are entertaining friends at home.

Despite what has become an untenable situation, Dan believes that he cannot deny any of Hank's requests, even though the job is exacting a heavy toll on his physical and emotional well-being and on his family life. Because he is so stressed by Hank and his unreasonable demands, Dan takes out his frustration on his own wife and son. Plagued by severe tension and migraine headaches, Dan knows that he has hair-trigger nerves. He feels strongly that Hank's children should be removed from their positions of responsibility and authority in the company. But he fears Hank's explosive temper and senses that any suggestion he makes along such lines might backfire and cost him his job.

Dan believes, with good basis, that his career alternatives are extremely limited. His position in the company has been earned by thirty years at Hank's side, starting as a clerk in the first store. Dan doubts that he could find another position of equal status and financial remuneration in another company, especially considering his lack of formal management training, his limited education, and his age. To make matters worse, Dan feels chronically insecure in his job. He has witnessed too many arbitrary dismissals of high-ranking and presumably valued executives in the company simply because Hank acted in a fit of irrational anger.

So, Dan sees no option other than to continue to withstand Hank's frequent furor, capricious demands, and manipulative exploitation. He knows that his relationship with Hank is the major cause of his emotional troubles—his restlessness, anxiety, frustration, and anger. But Dan fails to acknowledge how much the relationship threatens his physical health as well. At 3:00 A.M., as he dresses to leave on a search for one of Hank's missing sons, Dan mutters metaphorically, "This guy is gonna be the death of me." He might well be speaking the truth.

Louise and Robert are about to have yet another serious talk about their relationship. During the fourteen months that they have been together, they have broken up three times, all for the same reason: Robert seems unable to make the commitment to the relationship that Louise needs.

At 29, Louise already feels the ticking of her biological clock.

7

She was married once, briefly, in her early twenties; now, after seven years of single life, she is very ready to get married again. When Louise met Robert, a 35-year-old bachelor, at a friend's party, she was elated. He seemed perfect, and, at least at first, he was.

Louise and Robert's courtship took off in high gear. They spoke of marriage and children on their third date. Robert told her that he had never had a fully committed relationship, but that now he was truly ready to settle down and begin a family. They compared their family backgrounds, religious views, political attitudes, and dreams for the future. Everything looked right. And they loved each other in bed. Louise believed that, at long last, her dreams were about to come true.

But then, after only three months, Robert began to back off. He canceled dates with her; he made excuses to avoid making love; he became progressively less affectionate. When Louise confronted him, Robert explained that he was feeling frightened about making a commitment and "needed some time and space to work things out in my head."

Internally, Louise's anxiety meter hit the panic level. But she remained reasonably calm externally and agreed to a separation for a few weeks in order to give Robert the time and space he needed. She assured him that she would wait for him and wouldn't date anyone else.

When Robert called after two weeks, he told Louise that he loved her and wanted to make their relationship work. He asked that she be understanding of his fears and help him work out his anxieties. She agreed.

Then, two months later, the pattern repeated itself: Robert's coldness, avoidance of sex, unreliability in keeping dates, and, eventually, his need for "more space." This time, Louise handled the situation differently. Instead of consoling Robert and being understanding, she became angry, distant, and withdrawn from him. She informed him that if he couldn't make a commitment soon, she was going to start dating other men.

This time, Robert came back in only ten days. And he seemed more in love than ever. He was amorous in bed and affectionate in public. He apologized and promised that his fears would not overtake him again. He couldn't bear to lose her, he said, and insisted that "within a few months, I think I'll be ready to talk about marriage."

Louise was patient. She waited for eight months without raising the subject of marriage. Then, with her thirtieth birthday just around the corner, she broached the subject of commitment once again. This time, Robert responded with a list of reasons why he was fearful of getting married to her. He felt pressured, he said, and didn't want to feel "controlled by a woman." He worried about how compatible their personalities *really* were. He wondered about whether he was cut out to be the kind of husband she seemed to need.

They talked for hours. And, once again, they broke up. This time, Louise was furious. She accused Robert of wasting her time. She said she wasn't "so damn sure" about him either, that she hated "wishy-washy men," and that she wanted her children's father to "know his own mind."

When Robert started calling again after a month, he could only reach her answering machine. It seemed that Louise was out almost every night, and Robert became jealous. He sent flowers; he left funny messages; he was his most charming self. Louise finally softened.

Now, she is waiting for Robert to pick her up for a romantic dinner and the inevitable talk about the relationship. It is, she thinks, all getting a bit tiresome. Although she felt wonderful when Robert came back, her self-esteem is still hurting. Why is he so ambivalent about marrying her? Is there something wrong with her that he isn't saying? How can she trust that this time he will really mean it even if he says he wants to get married? Maybe he'll leave her anyway for another woman. Just thinking about it makes her stomach ache. In fact, the pain bothers her most of the time these days. She has even developed strange rashes and bad allergies. She heads to the medicine cabinet for her stomach medication, never once thinking that her relationship might well be the cause of all her physical distress.

9

Who Are Lethal Lovers?

Just about all of us can recognize the dangerousness of a spouse or lover who commits acts of physical violence and abuse. But this book is about relationships whose threat to the physical well-being of one or both partners is not overtly violent or explicitly physical. Instead, the danger in these relationships lies in the creation of insidious negative emotions that, over time, erode physical well-being and deteriorate emotional health. As you will see, lovers—male or female—whose behavior evokes toxic feelings in their partners can ultimately be as lethal as those who use a gun or a knife.

Your close relationships provide important information about the personalities of the people with whom you are intimately involved. At the same time, those relationships also function as the psychological mirrors that show you who *you* are. In this way, the manner in which you are treated in your intimate relationships directly affects your sense of self-worth and profoundly shapes the mental picture you have of yourself—that is, your self-concept. To a very considerable degree, you come to understand yourself through the experiences of your closest interpersonal bonds—initially, of those that were formed with your parents, and later, of the love relationships and other significant ties of adulthood.

Because you invest so much of your time and so many of your hopes and dreams in intimate relationships, how they work or turn out tremendously influences your entire worldview. How you feel about people in general, and men or women in particular, is affected by your experiences in love relationships. Whether you have positive, optimistic expectations about life or a negative, burned out, cynical outlook is determined largely by your positive or negative—reaffirming or disillusioning—experiences in love relationships.

A Lethal Lover, then, is a person whose behavior in a love relationship causes you to feel depressed, helpless, out of control, anxious, hostile, frustrated, cynical, or unable to cope. These are some of the psychological poisons produced by toxic relationships.

... And Other Toxic Relationships Harmful to Your Health

While psychological poisons are most prevalent and toxic in intimate love relationships, other types of significant relationships also can exert a highly negative impact on your health.

Because you may spend as much waking time—and often more—at work as you do at home, relationships in the workplace can seriously threaten your health when they create toxic emotions. As a general rule, the more "fate control" a person at work has over you, the greater his or her potential for causing you harm.

When your supervisor or boss acts in ways that make you feel anxious, angry, or insecure, the psychological and physical impact of such feelings will be determined by the degree of influence he or she exercises on your salary, promotions, and employment status. On the other hand, while subordinates or co-workers might be aggravating or frustrating, their impact on your fate at work is probably minimal, and their impact on your health is therefore less.

Relationships with parents, children, and close friends have many of the same qualities as close romantic ties in terms of their impact on your self-esteem and moods. Your parents were the initial mirrors that reflected your self-concept. If you were fortunate enough to have loving, approving, demonstrative parents, you probably derived a stronger sense of self-worth and confidence than did people whose parents were withholding, cold, inconsistent, or disapproving. The adult children of alcoholic parents, for example, continue to suffer the wounds to their self-esteem caused by dysfunctional parental behavior.

Let us turn now to some examples of the physiological mechanisms through which toxic relationships and negative emotions do their damage.

2

Psychological Poisons

After undergoing an hour's worth of probing, poking, and other diagnostic assault on her already tender stomach, Linda is dressing in her doctor's examining room and thinking once again about her marital problems. Her doctor has asked to speak with her in his office when she is ready.

As she takes a seat opposite his desk, Linda tries to avoid eye contact with him, fearful that her expression will give away the emotional pain she is feeling.

"Linda," he begins, "I'm genuinely concerned about you. Of course, I don't have any of the answers yet. We'll have to wait for the lab work. But I've got to tell you: I don't like what I see. You've been sick this year more than you've been well, and frankly, you seem quite depressed to me. I'm no psychologist, but I have a feeling that your emotional state may have a lot to do with your low resistance. Look, Linda, we're old friends. Is there anything I can do to help? Do you want to talk about anything?"

Linda feels the tears well up in her eyes. She is touched by

12

his concern, but at the same time she feels humiliated at being exposed. She feels transparent.

"I appreciate your concern," she responds. "I think I'm just down because I don't feel well, that's all." Then, after only a moment, Linda chokes back a sob. "No," she admits. "It's more than that . . . but there's nothing you can do. There's nothing anybody can do. I just have to get hold of myself. I feel so damned out of control."

"Okay," the doctor replies. "Now at least you're starting to talk about *some* kind of problem. I don't know what's going on and maybe it's not my business to know. But I think there are some things you can do—that you *need* to do—if you want to get well."

As he reaches for his prescription pad, Linda thinks, *Good. At least he's going to give me something to make me feel better.* She asks, "Will that help me sleep?"

The doctor's reply is unexpected. "No, Linda, I'm not writing you a prescription. At least not for medication. I'm giving you the name and telephone number of a psychologist that I want you to call. Will you do that much for me and for yourself?"

Linda feels herself sinking into an even deeper emotional hole. *Oh, this is great,* she thinks. *Now the doctor thinks I'm nuts.* Then she replies, with no enthusiasm, "Okay, I'll think about it."

Nearly two weeks after Linda's doctor called me to say that he had referred a patient for assessment and psychotherapy, Linda contacted me. We spoke on the phone about her resistance to the idea of seeing a psychologist. Her view, as she explained in that initial conversation, was that her *husband* was "messed up" and that she wasn't "the one who needs to see someone . . . *he* is."

However, when I suggested that she come in for at least one session in order for us to discuss how *her* feelings about her husband were very likely contributing to *her* health problems, both physical and emotional, she reluctantly agreed. That first session turned into a yearlong relationship between us, through which Linda has come to learn a great deal about the concept of Lethal Lovers and about what she could—and did, in fact—do to protect her health.

The story of how Linda came to be one of my patients is fairly typical in my practice. What it reflects, in part, is the profound revolution that has taken place in medical thinking over the last two decades with respect to the causes of illness and the paths to healing.

What Makes Us Sick?

The cutting edge of research on the causes of illness now emphasizes the key role played by our *minds*—our attitudes, moods, emotions, beliefs, and behavior—on the function or dysfunction of our *bodies*. This field of medical research is called psychoneuroimmunology, or PNI. In short, PNI is the study of how the mind affects the biochemistry of the brain and body and, in turn, how the biochemistry of the body and brain affect the mind.

Research in PNI shows, for example, that when people believe that life problems are beyond their control, the stress hormone cortisol increases in their bloodstream, thereby lowering the ability of their immune systems to effectively fight off bacterial and viral infections and, in severe cases, even some forms of cancer. Chronic and pervasive feelings of anxiety and/ or depression have been shown to have an adverse effect on immunity by depressing the function of what are called "natural killer cells"—cells that are activated to search and destroy foreign, dangerous invaders. When this function is diminished because the individual is psychologically depressed, he or she will necessarily become more vulnerable to illness, as Linda's health problems reflect. Further immune system compromise occurs when an individual views setbacks as catastrophes to which no effective coping response seems possible.[1]

Technically, another person's actions do not *directly* damage your physical health, except in obvious cases where there is a literal infliction of bodily harm. But what quite literally can kill you—or certainly make you vulnerable to a host of health problems—is *your negative reaction* to what that other person says or does, or *your negative reaction to your perception* of the relationship. Phenomena once believed to be purely psychological—thinking, feeling, or acting—now are known to be connected to actual physiological events in the body. Relationships, then, can become toxic by creating patterns of thought or behavior that produce potent psychological poisons.

From Germs to Stress to Toxic Emotions

As medical research advanced over the years—from early microbe hunters to today's laser gunslingers—one question continually puzzled scientists until fairly recently: Why do people who are exposed to the same germ or other threat of identical illness respond differently? In other words, why do some people become sick while others stay healthy?

The picture was obviously more complex than the one painted by initial researchers of germs and disease. Eventually, a multiple-cause theory emerged that is better able to account for the causes of illness. It states that several causes are at work simultaneously in illness, including not only exposure to foreign agents—germs, toxins, and the like—but also environment, age, genetic predisposition, health practices (such as diet, exercise patterns, smoking, or alcohol consumption), and emotional functioning, particularly as reflected by high levels of stress.

Of all the multiple causes put forth, *stress* provides the most popular explanation of why some individuals succumb to illness while others stay well. Being "stressed out" or "under a lot of stress" have become common phrases in our conversations with one another and with our doctors.

A Canadian endocrinologist, Dr. Hans Selye, is widely credited with being the first to describe the phenomenon of stress and to link it to the development of illness—specifically *psycho-*

somatic disorders. The stress concept has since enjoyed wide-spread prominence as researchers have accumulated compelling evidence that stress—in the form of major disruptive life events, inordinate demands, high-strung personality styles (e.g., Type A), or traumatic change—is correlated with a host of physical and psychological maladies.

Negative stress certainly makes one vulnerable to some form of breakdown, either physical or psychological. But what determines the breakdown is not so much the negative stress itself but (and this is key) your perception of whether the negative stress is essentially *out of your control* and, in the worst cases, entirely *overwhelming*.

Some stress, however, actually can be good for your health. This kind of stress can be described as an experience that is challenging, exciting, arousing, fun, or that gives life purpose and meaning. Positive stressful experiences, or events that you interpret as positive, do not make you sick. In fact, they have a lot to do with making and keeping you healthy. Since stress, in its most basic sense, is your body's way of adapting to the ongoing process of life itself, the absence of any stress—positive or negative—is not desirable. In fact, to paraphrase Hans Selye, without any stress at all you would, in a word, be dead.

The Secret of Psychological Hardiness

Research also shows that the very same stressful experience can have deleterious effects on one person while having neutral or even beneficial effects on another. An innovative study[2] conducted on two hundred top managers of the same company going through a stressful several-month period found that half of the subjects developed signs of diagnosable illness—but the other half seemed unfazed by the stress. Why?

The healthier executives responded to and interpreted the stressful events in three fundamentally different ways from those who became ill:

16

1. They viewed the stressful changes as a *challenge*.
2. They maintained a sense of *control* and optimism over the course of the stressful events ahead of them.
3. They exhibited a deep and abiding *commitment* to their work and to their lives generally.

Later studies with different groups, men and women, all showed the same results: Those who maintained good health had a greater sense of *control* over their lives and stressful circumstances; they felt a greater *commitment* to their work, family, and even to themselves; and they interpreted the stressful changes in their lives as opportunities for *challenge* and personal growth.

Thus, the hardy personality style has come to be known as embodying the three life-saving "C's": challenge, control, and commitment.

While exposure to stress remains a significant risk factor for many diseases, it is the individual's *response* to stress that makes the critical difference between whether or not illness occurs. In other words, your vulnerability or resistance to what ails you, to a significant extent, resides in your head.

The Mind-Body Connection

Only very recently have researchers begun to understand precisely how the psychological piece of the equation operates. Previously, the link between the mind and body was the subject of speculation and wonderment by believers, and denial or minimization by skeptics. However compelling the evidence of how a positive mental outlook helped one patient beat cancer, or of how another patient—by substituting a more relaxed, accepting mindset for an intense, pressured one—was able to reverse some symptoms of heart disease, it was still based only on doctors' clinical anecdotes.

Within the last several years, however, major technological advances have enabled scientists to unravel much of the mystery behind the perennial question of how the mind and body are connected. The evidence now indisputably shows that an exquisitely sensitive relationship exists between the thoughts, feelings, and beliefs that arise in your brain and the regulation of your body's major physiological systems. That link lies in biochemistry. In the presence of various emotional states, your brain releases powerful biochemical messengers that activate and regulate or overactivate and disregulate your immune system, cardiovascular system, and endocrine system. This, then, is the mechanism that explains how what goes on in your head can affect whether you will stay healthy or become ill.

For example, when you experience anger and hostility, large amounts of the stress hormone norepinephrine are secreted in your body. Over time, chronic hostility produces a hormonal excess that can lead to a dangerous buildup of plaque in your coronary arteries and veins. The excessive norepinephrine also causes high blood pressure. The elevated pressure and the eventual blockages that result from accumulated plaque can then produce heart attacks, strokes, and arteriosclerosis.[3]

On the positive side, good coping responses—primarily a sense of control—will cause the stress hormones to decrease. If you are able to maintain the mindset of psychological hardiness, feel satisfied with yourself and your life, and cultivate genuinely supportive personal relationships, you will be less likely to become sick. Good coping responses activate your body's natural built-in healing and protective capabilities.

The key point is that what goes on in your head, in terms of how you react to life situations and relationships—*in interaction with other risk factors*—greatly affects whether you resist or succumb to the stresses of life. Once you understand and accept how your *responses* to life directly impact the state of your physical and emotional health, you also will see the potential for very real damage to arise out of your unhealthy interactions with other people.

Your body's intricate biochemistry explains how negative emotional responses that arise from bad relationships produce psychological poisons that diminish the quality of your health. A difficult, unhappy relationship with a boyfriend or girlfriend, a taxing, draining, demoralizing marriage, or an infuriating relationship with a boss are not just the stuff of soap operas. When it's happening to you, it's deadly serious business.

To protect your health, you first need to recognize the signs that one of your close relationships has become toxic.

3

✖━━━━✖━━━━✖

What Is Your Relationship
Toxicity Level?

Y̲ou now are probably concerned that at least one of your significant relationships is posing a threat to your physical and emotional health. The questionnaire that follows will help you better ascertain the degree and nature of that threat by calculating your Relationship Toxicity Level—RTL.

The questionnaire is designed so that you may use it to measure toxicity in any type of relationship—romantic love, friendship, work, or familial. Naturally, you may use the questionnaire several times to evaluate different relationships.

There are four parts to the questionnaire. Part 1 directly assesses the emotional impact of your relationship by measuring the frequency and intensity of the Seven Deadly Signs of a Toxic Relationship. We will cover this in further detail in the next chapter.

Part 2 concerns your perception of the relationship. Using rating scales, it will ask you to describe the qualities of your relationship *from your perspective.* Do not worry about whether your perceptions are consistent with those of your partner or how an impartial, outside observer might evaluate the relationship. What matters here is how things appear from *your* vantage point.

Part 3 gives you an opportunity to describe your partner's personality traits, intentions, and behavior. Once again, it doesn't matter whether he or she would agree with or approve of your report. The level of toxicity in your relationship is based on how *you* are affected. In other words, the RTL reflects the extent to which *your* health is placed at risk.

Finally, part 4 measures your current stress-related symptoms.

When you complete the questionnaire, you will find instructions for scoring and interpretation. You should not consider the questionnaire a definitive or foolproof measure of toxicity in your relationship. Rather, the questionnaire is intended to sensitize you to the relative toxicity level your answers suggest and to the possibility that risk to your health might exist. In addition, knowing your RTL will heighten your awareness of the warning signs of toxicity in your relationship and alert you to the need for immediate corrective action.

The Relationship Toxicity
Level Questionnaire

Focus on a person with whom you have a relationship that causes you to have negative feelings. Each time the symbol (_____) appears in the questions below, substitute the name of the person in your relationship.

When answering, think about your feelings *during the past three months* of your relationship with this person. (Note: If the relationship is *less* than three months old, consider the total time that you have been involved; or, if you haven't seen or been involved with the person during the past three months, focus on the *last* three months of your involvement.)

Answer every question from the perspective of *your* experience. Do not worry about whether your answers are right or wrong, good or bad. Just be as honest and accurate as possible.

If a question concerns feelings or behavior that are clearly inappropriate or out of the range of normal interaction for the *type* of relationship on which you are focusing, simply write the letters "n/a" (not applicable) beside it and proceed to the next question. For example, issues of faithfulness do not usually apply to work relationships.

PART 1

1. How often do you feel helpless, overwhelmed, or out of control when there is a problem in your relationship or when (_____) does something that upsets you or makes you feel unhappy?

    1) never or almost never
    2) sometimes
    3) often
    4) most of the time
    5) always or almost always

2. How strong or intense are your feelings of helplessness, loss of control, or being overwhelmed?

    1) not strong at all
    2) somewhat strong
    3) very strong
    4) as strong as anything I have ever felt

3. How often do you feel anxious, insecure, or uncertain about (_____) and/or your relationship?

    1) never or almost never
    2) sometimes
    3) often
    4) most of the time
    5) always or almost always

4. How strong or intense are your feelings of anxiety, insecurity, or uncertainty?

    1) not strong at all
    2) somewhat strong

3) very strong

4) as strong as anything I have ever felt

5. How often do you feel angry, enraged, or irritable with (_____) and/or your relationship?

1) never or almost never

2) sometimes

3) often

4) most of the time

5) always or almost always

6. How strong or intense is your anger, rage, or irritability?

1) not strong at all

2) somewhat strong

3) very strong

4) as strong as anything I have ever felt

7. How often do you feel frustrated with (_____) and/or your relationship?

1) never or almost never

2) sometimes

3) often

4) most of the time

5) always or almost always

8. How strong or intense is your frustration?

1) not strong at all

2) somewhat strong

3) very strong

4) as strong as anything I have ever felt

9. How often do you feel cynical, jealous, distrustful, or pessimistic in response to (_____) and/or your relationship?

1) never or almost never

2) sometimes

3) often

4) most of the time

5) always or almost always

10. How strong are your feelings of cynicism, jealousy, distrust, or pessimism?

1) not strong at all
2) somewhat strong
3) very strong
4) as strong as anything I have ever felt

11. How often do you feel bad about yourself—down on your self-esteem, confidence, self-image—in response to (_____) and/or your relationship?
1) never or almost never
2) sometimes
3) often
4) most of the time
5) always or almost always

12. How strong are your negative feelings about yourself?
1) not strong at all
2) somewhat strong
3) very strong
4) as strong as anything I have ever felt

13. How often do you feel hopeless, depressed, or despairing about (_____) and/or your relationship?
1) never or almost never
2) sometimes
3) often
4) most of the time
5) always or almost always

14. How strong are your feelings of hopelessness, depression, or despair?
1) not strong at all
2) somewhat strong
3) very strong
4) as strong as anything I have ever felt

PART 2

Think about your relationship with (_____). Each of the rating scales below shows two polar-opposite adjectives connected by a 7-point scale. For each scale, circle the number from 1 to 7 that best describes where *your relationship* fits between the two adjectives.

warm	1 2 3 4 5 6 7	cold
communicative	1 2 3 4 5 6 7	uncommunicative
interesting	1 2 3 4 5 6 7	boring
respectful	1 2 3 4 5 6 7	demeaning
supportive	1 2 3 4 5 6 7	unsupportive
comforting	1 2 3 4 5 6 7	agitating
understandable	1 2 3 4 5 6 7	confusing
safe	1 2 3 4 5 6 7	threatening
honest	1 2 3 4 5 6 7	dishonest
close	1 2 3 4 5 6 7	distant
relaxing	1 2 3 4 5 6 7	stressful
accepting	1 2 3 4 5 6 7	rejecting
flexible	1 2 3 4 5 6 7	rigid
satisfying	1 2 3 4 5 6 7	unsatisfying
reliable	1 2 3 4 5 6 7	unreliable
liberating	1 2 3 4 5 6 7	controlling
positive	1 2 3 4 5 6 7	negative
fulfilling	1 2 3 4 5 6 7	draining

| compatible | 1 2 3 4 5 6 7 | incompatible |
| happy | 1 2 3 4 5 6 7 | sad |

PART 3

The rating scales below refer to the personality traits and behavior of (_____). Again, circle the number from 1 to 7 that best fits (_____).

loyal	1 2 3 4 5 6 7	disloyal
kind	1 2 3 4 5 6 7	cruel
patient	1 2 3 4 5 6 7	impatient
empathic	1 2 3 4 5 6 7	unempathic
loving	1 2 3 4 5 6 7	callous
accepting	1 2 3 4 5 6 7	critical
sensitive	1 2 3 4 5 6 7	insensitive
trustworthy	1 2 3 4 5 6 7	untrustworthy
affectionate	1 2 3 4 5 6 7	unaffectionate
giving	1 2 3 4 5 6 7	withholding

PART 4

In the blank that precedes each item listed below, rate how often you experienced the problem during the past three months of your relationship with (_____). Mark a **3** if you had the problem frequently; a **2** if you had the problem sometimes; a **1** if you had the problem rarely; and a **0** if you have not had the problem at all.

_____ Headache

_____ Feelings of nervousness or tension

_____ Feelings of being hurried, rushed, or pressured

_____ Backache; muscle spasm or pain in back, neck, or shoulders

_____ Pain in face or jaw; teeth grinding or clenching

_____ Fatigue or exhaustion

_____ Feelings of being down, blue, or depressed

_____ Intoxication from overuse of alcohol or other drugs

_____ Feelings of "burnout" or depletion

_____ Skin rashes or disorders

_____ Sleep difficulties

_____ Appetite disturbances (loss or unusual increase)

_____ Temper outbursts or irritability

_____ Feelings of being overwrought or "strung out"

_____ Chest pains, tightness or pressure on the chest

_____ Shortness of breath

_____ Allergies

_____ Nervous stomach, intestinal pains, indigestion

_____ Bowel irregularity

_____ Colds, flus, respiratory infections

_____ Feelings of worry and insecurity

_____ Eye strain or sore eyes

_____ Dizziness or nausea

_____ Inflamed, painful, or swollen joints

HOW TO SCORE AND INTERPRET YOUR ANSWERS

Scoring Part 1. Fill in the numerical value of your answers for each question in the format below. For example, if your answer to question 1 was "most of the time," fill in a score of **4** in the space indicated; if your answer to question 2 was "somewhat strong," fill in the number **2**.

When you have filled in the appropriate scores for each question, multiply your answers as directed. Multiply your score on question 1 by your score on question 2 in order to compute your "Helplessness Factor." Continue these calculations for all seven factors.

Helplessness Factor: Q1 _____ × Q2 _____ = _____
Anxiety Factor: Q3 _____ × Q4 _____ = _____
Hostility Factor: Q5 _____ × Q6 _____ = _____
Frustration Factor: Q7 _____ × Q8 _____ = _____
Cynicism Factor: Q9 _____ × Q10 _____ = _____
Self-Esteem Factor: Q11 _____ × Q12 _____ = _____
Hopelessness Factor: Q13 _____ × Q14 _____ = _____
TOTAL = _____

Total your factor scores (the multiplied values). Then, divide your total by 7. This will give you your *Deadly Sign Score*:

Total _____ ÷ 7 = _____ = *Deadly Sign Score*

Now interpret your level of risk and determine your **Deadly Sign Index** from the table below. Your Deadly Sign Score will range from a low of 1 to a high of 20. The table gives you the relative risk level of your score and your corresponding **Deadly Sign Index.** The level of risk reflects how much your emotional reactions might imperil your physical and emotional health.

Deadly Sign Score	Level of Risk	Deadly Sign Index
1 to 3	Almost no risk	1
4 to 7	Low risk	2
8 to 13	Moderate risk	3
14 to 20	High risk	4

Scoring Part 2. Total your numeric scores for each of the rating scales. Then, divide your total by 20 to arrive at your *Relationship Negativity Factor.* (Note: If you omitted items because they were not applicable to the type of relationship you are evaluating, subtract the number of items marked "n/a" from 20; then divide your total score by the adjusted number.)

Total of numeric scores of all rating scales = _____
Total ____ ÷ 20 (or adjusted number) =
Relationship Negativity Factor

Now, interpret your score and determine your **Relationship Negativity Index** from the table below, which shows the degree of negative impact that your relationship has on you. Refer to the table to determine your **Relationship Negativity Index** for your score. Your Relationship Negativity Factor will range from 1 to 7.

Relationship Negativity Factor	Degree of Impact	Relationship Negativity Index
1	None	1
2 to 3	Low to moderate	2
4 to 5	Moderate to high	3
6 to 7	Very high	4

Scoring Part 3. Total your numeric scores on each of the rating scales. Then, divide your total by 10. (Note: If you omitted questions, subtract the total of "n/a" items from 10; then divide your total score by the adjusted number.) This will give you your *Partner Negativity Factor.* Your Partner Negativity Factor will range from 1 to 7.

Total of numeric scores = _____

Total ____ ÷ 10 (or adjusted number) = *Partner Negativity Factor*

To interpret the degree of negative impact that your partner has on you and to assign your **Partner Negativity Index,** refer to the table below.

29

Partner Negativity Factor	Degree of Impact	Partner Negativity Index
1	Low	1
2 to 3	Low to moderate	2
4 to 5	Moderate to high	3
6 to 7	Very high	4

Scoring Part 4. To arrive at your *Stress Symptom Factor,* simply add up your numeric scores for each item. Your Stress Symptom Factor will range from 0 to 72.

Symptom Factor = Total of numeric scores = _____

To determine your **Stress Symptom Index** and to interpret your level of possible stress-related symptoms, refer to the table below.

Stress Symptom Factor	Level of Symptomatology	Stress Symptom Index
0 to 15	Very low to low	1
16 to 30	Low to moderate	2
31 to 49	Moderate to high	3
50 to 72	High to very high	4

HOW TOXIC IS YOUR RELATIONSHIP?

The final step is to calculate your **Relationship Toxicity Level— your RTL.** While each part of this questionnaire has given you a separate interpretation of the severity or risk reflected by your scores, the **RTL** provides an overall indication of the toxicity level in your relationship.

30

To determine your **RTL,** merely add your four *index* scores:

RTL =

    Your Deadly Sign Index   _____
plus Your Relationship Negativity Index   + _____
plus Your Partner Negativity Index   + _____
plus Your Stress Symptom Index   + _____

              TOTAL =   _____

Then, divide your total by 4.

             Total _____ ÷ 4 = RTL

Your **RTL** will range from 4 to 16. The level of toxicity in your relationship can be interpreted as follows:

RTL Score	Relationship Toxicity Level
4–5	Relatively safe
6–8	Low to moderate risk
9–12	Moderate to high risk
13+	Danger zone

You now have ascertained the toxicity level of your significant relationship or relationships. But, how did these negative patterns develop? As you will see in the next two chapters, there are Seven Deadly Signs of a Toxic Relationship which you and your partner have conditioned in each other through an ingrained and perilous sequence of action and reaction.

4

The Seven Deadly Signs
of a Toxic Relationship

Now that you have measured your Relationship Toxicity Level, it is important to understand more fully some of the causes and consequences of your toxic emotions. To begin with, if you know what to look for, your feelings will tell you if you are involved in a toxic relationship.

Intuitively, you may have long suspected that one or more of your relationships is brewing psychological poisons. Until now, though, you probably haven't realized the extent to which those negative emotions may be placing your physical health in peril.

There are Seven Deadly Signs that indicate toxicity in a relationship. Each sign refers to a persistent pattern of negative emotions that you feel *in response to your partner or relationship.* They are "deadly" signs because each is known to have damaging and potentially lethal physical and/or psychological consequences.

If your score on part 1 of the questionnaire was a 3 or 4, or if you identify your feelings with one or more of the following

Seven Deadly Signs of a toxic relationship, your health—your *life*—could be at risk:

1. Helplessness
2. Anxiety
3. Hostility
4. Frustration
5. Cynicism
6. Loss of self-esteem
7. Hopelessness

Negative emotional patterns represented by these seven signs are not confined to love relationships. They are also commonly found in work relationships, friendships, and family ties. However, when the deadly signs occur in the context of a romantic relationship, the damage potential is greater because of the intimacy and vulnerability that are involved. To the extent that your partner in a love relationship frequently provokes one or more of the deadly signs in you—*intentionally or unintentionally*—he or she is a Lethal Lover.

These deadly signs are emotional "buttons" that your partner pushes in you. This means that aspects of your partner's behavior, feelings, or attitudes typically elicit negative responses from you. These, in turn, trigger further provocative moves from your partner. In this way, your relationship is actually conditioning both of you to repeat a psychologically dangerous chain of action and reaction that, over time, will become more entrenched, more toxic, and more difficult to change.

The psychological poisons in toxic relationships are created by *chronic* patterns of the Seven Deadly Signs experienced over time. Thus, an *occasional* expression of anger, a *periodic* argument, a *transient* spell of depression or low self-esteem, or a *temporary* bout of anxiety may not indicate that your relationship is toxic.

But if you experience the deadly signs on a frequent, perhaps even chronic, basis, and your emotional reactions are relatively intense, your relationship is indeed toxic. Furthermore, it is unlikely that you will experience only one of the Seven Deadly Signs. This is because the emotional repercussions of one set of feelings are likely to trigger one or several other patterns of negative reactions. Since the signs are interrelated in this way, a highly toxic relationship usually generates a vicious cycle of negativity in which you may feel hopelessly caught.

Now, let's take a closer look at each of the Seven Deadly Signs.

The First Deadly Sign: Helplessness

Helplessness refers to an emotional tailspin that occurs when you have trouble coping.

In a tailspin, you experience a pervasive sense of being out of control or of having lost control of yourself and the problems in your relationship. This loss of control affects other areas of your life beyond the relationship. These might include your ability to discipline your personal health habits such as eating, drinking, exercising, or smoking; or you might be prone to excessive emotional reactions such as crying jags or temper outbursts; or your ability to focus and concentrate may be compromised.

The tailspin makes you feel overwhelmed and unable to cope effectively with your problems. It produces the perception that you are trapped in a bad situation with few or no alternatives and that you are helpless to make yourself feel better. As a result, you might try to escape the overwhelming problems by sleeping excessively, using drugs or alcohol to numb the pain, or using denial or avoidance strategies to shut out the sensation that you are drowning in your problems.

Naturally, these ineffective and self-destructive ways of coping only make you feel deeply disappointed, perhaps even disgusted with yourself. Your perception of your future is darkened, and your view of life in general becomes sour. This combination of feelings results in depression.

Helplessness may also reflect the underlying power structure of your relationship. If your partner exercises unilateral control over you and of the relationship, or harshly or constantly criticizes you or attacks your competence, your sense of inadequacy and helplessness will be reinforced.

The emotional tailspin can have far-reaching and potentially very harmful effects on your immune and cardiovascular systems. Prolonged feelings of helplessness activate excessive secretions of the stress hormone cortisol, interfering with your immune system's ability to fight bacteria, viruses, and environmental toxins, and to screen out renegade cells that might develop into cancer. Feeling overwhelmed and out of control can present particularly serious risks if you already have an underlying vulnerability to autoimmune diseases such as diabetes or rheumatoid arthritis.

Losing control over your eating, drinking, smoking, drug use, or exercise habits not only has detrimental health consequences, it also worsens feelings of helplessness.

Finally, chronic helplessness can trigger a worrisome biochemical imbalance by depleting your brain's supply of a chemical called *dopamine*, which produces symptoms of depression.

The Second Deadly Sign: Anxiety

Anxiety is comprised of negative emotional responses that include insecurity, fear, and uncertainty manifested as nervousness and tension. This often occurs when you are unable to predict or accurately anticipate either the behavior and feelings of your partner or the course of the relationship itself.

Anxiety is fueled by fears of abandonment and reinforced by the malfunction of the relationship. When a relationship fails to provide the reassurance, stability, and commitment necessary to calm uncertainty, toxic anxiety results. If, for example, your partner cannot or will not make a commitment to your love relationship—assuming a commitment is desired—your anxiety can go sky high. Without the predictability that commitment provides, the relationship can make you feel intensely vulnerable, exposed, and frightened. When anxiety levels escalate too much, loss of control is triggered.

Some people confuse predictability and stability with boredom. In relationships, they create drama, chaos, crises, and other uncertainties in order to keep themselves stimulated and interested. If your partner behaves in this way, the impact on you will be high levels of stress, anxiety, insecurity, and tension. Moreover, your fears of being abandoned or rejected will be constantly stimulated. Not only does this kind of partner wreak havoc with your health and peace of mind, but the relationship has a poor prognosis for longevity.

Chronic feelings of anxiety can damage your health in many ways. Protracted anxiety depresses the function of your immune system's natural killer cells designed to fight bacterial and viral infections. Tension and nervousness often produce headaches (including migraines), muscular and digestive disorders, exacerbations of painful arthritic conditions, diabetes and other immune or autoimmune diseases, numerous skin disorders, and many other maladies.

Anxiety is itself an emotional disorder and is closely related to depression. Protracted anxiety, caused by an unpredictable, unstable, or capricious relationship, triggers helplessness, loss of control, and clinical depression.

Strong anxiety can also predispose you to engage in harmful health practices such as abuse of alcohol, tranquilizers, or other drugs in a misguided attempt to calm yourself down. Abusing drugs and/or alcohol only creates further problems, which, in turn, become reason to feel out of control and depressed.

Finally, anxiety is a causal factor in many eating disorders and weight control problems. Cravings for sweets and other high carbohydrate junk foods are known to be stimulated by anxiety. The resultant weight gain and inevitable mood crash from "sugar highs" trigger further depression and still greater anxiety.

The Third Deadly Sign: Hostility

Hostility typically takes the form of aggression, anger, rage, and irritability. A partner or relationship to which you respond with hostility on a frequent or chronic basis is bad for your health. If you're always ready for a fight, you may well be on your way to a heart attack, too.

Overt hostility involves raising your voice, saying hurtful, angry words to your partner, accusing or blaming your partner of some "wrong," or in other ways openly conveying that your state of mind toward your partner is one of conflict and aggression rather than harmony and tranquility. In extreme cases, actual physical violence occurs.

It is not necessary, however, to display hostility openly in order to suffer its harmful physical and psychological effects. Hidden resentment, plotted revenge, and private negative fantasies that involve your partner are examples of covert hostility. The hostility may also become internalized—inappropriately directed against yourself in the form of guilt or depression. Covert hostility is likely to occur if you are intimidated by or fearful of your partner.

Hostility also is a common reaction to frustration, exploitation, manipulation, jealousy, betrayal, and devaluation, and is likely to result when any of the other deadly signs are provoked.

Hostility is a pernicious emotion that can wreak serious psychological and physical havoc on you and your partner. Of all the emotions that researchers have examined, the link between hostility and its physiological consequences is best understood. Almost two decades of research have clearly isolated hostility as *the* lethal quality most closely associated with heart and vascular disease in aggressive people.[4] The mechanism through which hostility exerts it heavy toll is a built-in, primitive stress reaction known as "fight or flight."

When this response is overactivated by chronic hostility, the excess stress hormone that is secreted damages the lining of your coronary arteries, creates a repeated chemical insult to your heart muscle, promotes high blood pressure, and disturbs your platelets and red blood cells. As a consequence, too much hostility over a sustained period of time results in a heightened risk of heart attack and other cardiovascular disease. Furthermore, the constant stimulation of the potent fight-or-flight response can trigger a massive coronary artery spasm leading to a major—and potentially fatal—heart attack.

Covert hostility, particularly chronically unexpressed anger, is damaging, too. Over time, the long-suppressed anger eventually boils over and explodes. Moreover, to the extent that you suppress your negative emotions—particularly rage—you run the risk of breaking down a critical function of your immune system that screens renegade cells. Such a breakdown makes you more vulnerable to cancer. Research also has shown that emotional suppression may put you at greater risk for high cholesterol, AIDS, and a range of other infectious and contagious illnesses.[5]

The Fourth Deadly Sign: Frustration

Frustration occurs when the gratification or fulfillment of any of your significant psychological or physical needs is obstructed. The longer your significant emotional needs remain unfulfilled, the more intense they will grow and the more toxic your frustration will become.

Continual frustration of your significant needs invariably will generate feelings of anger, resentment, and, eventually, outrage. Despite your attempts to control, deny, or rationalize your ire, it eventually will be aroused if your partner (or the relationship) fails to satisfy your needs for affection, sex, attention, acceptance, approval, reassurance, praise, or any other emotional requirements. Poor communication can be a major source of frustration—and eventual hostility—in relationships. When communication breaks down, your ability to discuss and resolve your problems is impaired. As a result, your relationship may be plagued by repetitive cycles of conflict over the same issues, causing further feelings of helplessness and futility. Hostility leads back to frustration and a dangerous cycle is established.

Even if your hostility remains submerged along with other unexpressed negative emotions, frustration still will result. With no expressive outlet, the internal buildup of frustration and anger can produce symptoms of depression and anxiety and numerous physical disorders.

The Fifth Deadly Sign: Cynicism

Jealousy, mistrust, suspicion, and disdain are characteristic components of the cynical reaction style.

Cynicism frequently occurs as a result of disillusioning and disappointing experiences with love. The nature of the love may be romantic, platonic, or familial. A friend who betrays you or a lover who abuses your trust undermines your willingness to rely on other people and to believe that their intentions toward you will be benevolent or even benign. Consequently, you may become depressed and pessimistic about life, love, and other people altogether. This overgeneralized reaction can be developed consciously as a protective mechanism. You may believe, for example, that by not trusting anyone, you will effectively defend yourself against further disillusionment or hurt. Sadly, though, your alienation and estrangement from intimate, trusting relationships only compounds your pain.

Cynicism can become a self-fulfilling prophecy. Either you will gravitate toward partners who lack integrity because their behavior is consistent with your negative beliefs, or you will actually create untrustworthy behavior in your partner because of your negative expectations. When you continually expect your partner to lie, cheat, or disappoint you, he or she is placed in the unenviable position of trying to prove innocence in the face of assumed guilt. If you expect the worst from your partner, he or she may eventually give up trying to prove you wrong and consequently conform his or her behavior to your cynical expectations—making your worst fears come true.

By harboring cynical emotions and expectations, you may also set the stage for your own self-destructive preemptive actions. This means that you might wind up doing the very behavior you fear or suspect in your partner *before* he or she does it to you. Thus, if you believe that your partner ultimately will abandon you, you might be the one to end the relationship even though no real evidence exists to substantiate your fears. Similarly, if you expect your partner to betray you through infidelity, you might become the one to stray, in a misguided attempt to protect your self-esteem. These preemptive actions, in turn, merely raise the toxicity level of your relationships and further entrench your already cynical belief system.

Cynicism triggers depression, anxiety, and loss of self-esteem, and while cynicism and negativity will surely sicken your soul, they can do considerable damage to your physical health as well. Negative thinking fuels negative moods. The chronic psychological depression that results from cynicism reflects itself in the literal depression of your immune system, making you vulnerable to contagious and infectious illnesses, as well as to cancer.

Cynicism, hostility, and mistrust also comprise the toxic core of the coronary-prone personality. This poisonous trio of emotions not only will harden your heart in a figurative sense, but literally will set in motion the biochemical process of hardening the arteries via high blood pressure and the building up of plaque.

The Sixth Deadly Sign: Loss of Self-Esteem

This sign includes feelings of diminished self-worth, inadequacy, negative self-image, reduced self-confidence, and deterioration of self-respect, with associated depression. When you acknowledge that you are choosing to stay in—or failing to leave—a relationship in which you feel devalued in significant ways, your self-esteem necessarily declines.

Impaired self-esteem is both a cause and a consequence of unhealthy relationships. If your sense of self-worth has been damaged as a result of a dysfunctional family background or other early experience, you might choose—albeit unconsciously—a similarly dysfunctional adult relationship or partner to confirm your negative self-image.

Your self-esteem also will suffer as a result of participating in a relationship in which you feel unappreciated, unloved, unworthy, and mistreated. Several factors contribute to this loss.

First, the recognition that you have involved yourself in a relationship that is unhealthy will undermine your confidence in your judgment. Then, having realized your error, you may try to undo or correct it by attempting to change your partner or to "fix" the relationship. To the extent that your efforts yield little or no success, your self-esteem is likely to further deteriorate. In your eyes, you have compounded the initial mistake by your inadequate efforts to make the relationship better.

Your self-esteem further erodes the longer you stay in a devaluing relationship. In order to rationalize your continued involvement, you may adopt a dangerous syllogism: People get what they deserve; you are being treated in ways that make you unhappy; therefore, you *deserve* to be unhappy.

This faulty reasoning leads you to accept your negative relationship on the grounds that you neither deserve nor can expect a better one. Consequently, your sense of helplessness increases and your self-esteem declines even more. With the progressive loss of self-confidence, your motivation either to improve your situation or to muster the courage to leave is sabotaged.

A particularly insidious and confusing erosion of your self-esteem occurs when you are the object of another person's ambivalence. When your partner simply can't seem to make up his or her mind about you, the unavoidable psychological message to your self-esteem is that, for whatever reasons, you are just not good enough.

Loss of self-esteem is closely related to each of the other deadly signs and, consequently, poses similar risks to your physical health. And, by definition, it is emotionally injurious, since positive, solid self-esteem is deemed a core criterion of good mental health.

The Seventh Deadly Sign: Hopelessness

This mosaic of despair, futility, and despondency is perhaps the most lethal of all the deadly signs. The numbing depression these emotions produce debilitates your motivation and distorts your thinking, thereby darkening your entire outlook on life and the future.

Your state of mind leads you to believe that your relationship and/or your life situation will never improve, or that it's impossible for you to feel better. This deadly attitude, known as the "giving up/given up" complex, has been isolated as the most consistent psychological precursor to a wide range of serious, often fatal illnesses. Of course, when depression bottoms out into hopelessness, the risk of suicide is high.

How does the giving up/given up complex operate to create susceptibility to illness and/or to make those whose health is already damaged become even more ill? The mechanism rests with the effects of depression and despair on brain biochemistry. When people are depressed, one of the brain's key chemical messengers that regulates other bodily functions, *catecholamine*, becomes severely depleted. The decline is sensed by the immune system, which, in turn, decreases its activity. It is this lowering of the immune system that makes depressed individuals more likely to become ill. To the extent that the individual is already ill, the depressed immune system fails to defeat invader pathogens.

When you have made repeated efforts in vain to talk with your partner, change your relationship, or alter your negative feelings, a profound sense of futility may envelop you. Your perception that things are hopeless—or very nearly—and that no viable options to your misery exist, however, is largely due to the protracted stress of your negative feelings.

This stress constricts your thinking so that only a few limited alternatives, if any, can be imagined. Your grim outlook makes whatever options you do imagine seem undesirable, thereby creating a psychological paralysis. You do not feel hopeless because there are no solutions; rather, you *perceive* that there are no solutions precisely *because* you feel stressed, hopeless, and depressed.

Giving up and allowing yourself feelings of despondency and hopelessness is the most dangerous choice you can make—and it *is* a choice. When you choose to give up, chemicals transmitted from your brain through your body carry the same message. If your immune and cardiovascular systems continue to receive that message, they may give up trying to keep you alive.

5

Dangerous Dancing

Together, Louise and Robert are doing a dangerous psychological dance around the issue of commitment. When Louise moves one step forward, Robert moves two steps back. But if Louise takes two steps back, Robert wants to move forward. Louise, it seems, is more appealing to Robert when she is dating other men; when Louise is committed to him, Robert becomes bored, nervous, and withdrawn.

This dance is dangerous for many reasons. First, of course, it is getting both of them nowhere quickly. While they may be dancing around commitment, so far their relationship is just standing still. Louise's biological clock is ticking louder, while Robert's attachment to his bachelorhood shows no signs of cracking. Even more dangerous is the fact that their psychological dance is addictive.

Neither Louise nor Robert is happy when they are apart, at least not for long. When the relationship is going well, the sexual chemistry between them is great. They have fun together and they feel comfortable. Both have been unable to find anyone else to capture their interest during separation periods.

Nevertheless, their intimacy invariably triggers Robert's ambivalence, at which point he feels compelled to distance himself from Louise. Although his ambivalence provokes Louise to date other men, he hates it when she does. Robert becomes depressed and lonely without her. He craves Louise like an addict craves his fix. When the pain of separation becomes nearly intolerable, Robert convinces himself that his depression is clear evidence of his deep love for Louise and he sets about to win her back. When he succeeds, he's euphoric . . . for a while.

The separations from Robert are equally painful for Louise. At first, the anger and hurt she feels at being devalued by his ambivalence helps strengthen her resolve to date other men. But, despite her efforts, her heart belongs to Robert. She, too, craves him when they are apart. But she stays away because she knows, from experience, that her avoidance of him and her threat to date other men comprise the formula that gets him back. And when Robert finally calls, lavishly remonstrating his love, she feels great . . . for a while.

Teaching Each Other to Dance

There are at least hundreds of thousands of Roberts and Louises out there doing the same dangerous dance in one form or another. Every psychotherapist I know has many female patients who, like Louise, are involved in frustrating, repetitive, addictive cycles of breaking up and reuniting, and trying to elicit commitments from men who seem incapable of making them.

The case of Louise and Robert illustrates a basic point about close relationships: A relationship is a unit of action and reaction, in which the partners condition each other into patterns of behavior, thoughts, and feelings.

Psychologically, the term *condition* means that behavior, thoughts, and feelings are learned through the connection of a stimulus, a response, and a reinforcement. Simply put, a stimulus is anything that one partner does that elicits a response in the other. In turn, the response of the second partner becomes the stimulus for the first partner to respond again. That is how the sequence of actions and reactions is established.

For example, when Robert withdraws emotionally, his behavior is the stimulus for Louise to respond by becoming angry, upset, and, on her part, also rejecting. Louise's response, in turn, becomes a new stimulus for eliciting Robert's depression. So it goes in a seemingly endless chain of behaviors, each of which functions as both stimulus and response in the cycle.

The most important part of the dance is the *reinforcement*. Without it, the chain of responses would be broken. A reinforcement is anything that occurs right after a response that increases its likelihood of occurring again.

When Louise and Robert first met, their advances toward each other—shows of affection, self-disclosure, statements of their interest—were reinforced. When Robert kissed Louise, she kissed him back; Louise's reciprocated affection reinforced Robert's kiss. Similarly, when Louise told Robert that he was the best man she had ever met, he smiled and stroked her cheek; Louise consequently was reinforced for her self-disclosures by Robert's expression of affection. At first, the relationship was on an entirely positive keel.

The relationship took its first negative turn when Robert pulled back emotionally. At first, Louise's response was to quash her anxiety and to reassure Robert that he could take all the time and space necessary to assuage his fears. So, he was reinforced for his distancing actions by Louise's understanding and patience.

Eventually, though, Louise responded to Robert's emotional reversals with anger. Now, here's where the relationship begins to turn toxic: Robert's behavior actually is reinforced more by Louise's anger. When she breaks up with him in anger, Robert's fear of commitment and marriage is *immediately* alleviated. Since the removal of a negative feeling is a reinforcement,

Louise's angry actions initially increase the strength of Robert's emotional withdrawal response. But, during their separation, both become depressed. Then, their addictive pattern is further reinforced when their reconciliation ceases the pain of being apart.

Reinforcements and "White Door" Behavior

There are two kinds of reinforcements: positive and negative.

Positive reinforcement is what we generally mean by the term *reward*. A pat on the head, a hug, a "good boy!" or "good girl!" are the reinforcements with which most of us were raised. Later in life, our habit patterns are shaped and reinforced by more "adult" reinforcers such as money, sex, love, popularity, status, and the like.

Psychologists have long used laboratory animals to draw human analogies. In a classic illustration of positive and negative reinforcement, a white rat is placed in a black cage containing a white door. The rat discovers that cheese awaits him if he passes through the white door. Soon, whenever the rat is placed in the black cage, he makes a beeline for the white door and the cheese. The cheese is positive reinforcement for his going through the white door.

Louise and Robert used a lot of positive reinforcers in their initial "falling in love" phase. But then they began to use negative reinforcement—albeit inadvertently—when Robert's ambivalence started. Negative reinforcement is *not* the same thing as punishment.

Negative reinforcement is illustrated with a second rat placed in the black cage, who is subjected to electric shocks. But the shocks cease as soon as he escapes through the white door. No cheese, just no pain. The cessation of pain becomes itself a potent reward. By this form of negative reinforcement, the rat quickly becomes conditioned to run immediately through the white door.

Learning through negative reinforcement is called "aversive conditioning." Louise and Robert run each other through several courses of negative reinforcement and aversive conditioning. When Louise begins to pressure Robert about making a commitment, Robert experiences her behavior as a negative stimulus: It causes him fear and anxiety. In response, Robert pulls back emotionally from Louise. This, in turn, provokes a confrontation that ends in the breakup of the relationship. Robert's emotional distancing, therefore, is reinforced because it immediately produces an escape from the aversive pressure Louise exerts and the uncomfortable feelings her demands create.

However, in short order, the stakes are raised. Within days, Robert begins to suffer the pain of separation from Louise. His anxiety and fear about commitment are now replaced by even worse feelings: depression, loneliness, and addictive panic that he may have lost her forever. After a few painful weeks, his jealousy and depression become overwhelming. Now the pressure is really on. The shock grids are turned up to high voltage: Robert must get out of the separation pain he feels. So, he calls Louise, proclaims his love, and promises to make a commitment. In this way, he runs through his proverbial white door to the cessation of separation and withdrawal pain.

On her part, Louise's behavior is negatively reinforced when the pain of her anger and lowered self-esteem is stopped—albeit temporarily—by Robert's protestations of undying love. But, after the dust settles and the immediate crisis passes, of course, the dangerous dance will start over again.

A Tale of Two Pigeons

The schedule or pattern of reinforcement that is used to shape behavior is as important as the type of reinforcement.

Again, the point is well illustrated in a psychology laboratory. This time, the subjects are two hungry pigeons. The first pigeon eventually discovers that each time he presses a lever, he receives a food pellet in his trough. One push, one pellet. This is known as *continuous* reinforcement.

A second pigeon begins his discovery the same way. But

soon the game changes for him. Now, instead of 100 percent continuous reinforcement, the food is delivered on a *partial* or *intermittent* basis. Sometimes he gets a pellet, sometimes he doesn't. (This is also known as a "gambling schedule," and you can see it occur whenever you watch human "pigeons" at a slot machine.)

The test of addiction comes when suddenly *all* food is withheld from *both* pigeons. In short order, pigeon 1 stops pushing the lever and exhibits no signs of addiction-like behavior. But pigeon 2 *continues* to push the lever over and over to the point of literal collapse—hoping for another pellet just the way he received it on the intermittent schedule. This is conditioned addictive behavior.

The lesson of the pigeons is profoundly important in that it explains why, as a human "pigeon," you may continue holding on to a relationship that long ago stopped being rewarding. If you got "hooked" on that relationship because the rewards came intermittently and then with very little or no predictability, you could well be dangerously addicted to the relationship.

Once you have established a relationship "habit"—like pigeon 2's lever-pressing habit—on the basis of an intermittent reinforcement schedule, it becomes exceedingly difficult to discern when the right time has come to give up the habit and quit the relationship. Instead, like pigeon 2, you might continue to exert yourself in futile or counterproductive efforts to make the relationship pay off, to the point that you endure both physical and psychological damage.

Perhaps the most telling lesson of the pigeon story is that addictive behavior can be conditioned in creatures who lack a cerebral cortex, that evolved and complex cognitive apparatus of human beings that allows us to conjure such concepts as hope, faith, love, belief, and so on. Thus, the addictive behavior observed in the pigeons is purely conditioned—reflex actions to stimuli with which reinforcements, at some point, were associated.

What this suggests is that at least some of the psychologically dangerous interaction in which people participate may not be the result either of rational thinking or of being "in love." On the contrary, it may be simple conditioning. But the good news is that *learned* behavior can be *unlearned*.

Dangerous Dancing Lessons

Every relationship is a *unit* of interaction in which each partner's behavior serves as both stimulus and reinforcement to the behavior of the other. Because of this, partners are capable of conditioning each other to behave in certain ways. The manner in which this is done—which reinforcements are used for which specific behaviors—varies from couple to couple, or relationship to relationship, and may or may not be conscious. Nevertheless, ritualized patterns of interaction are created—habitual ways of responding to each other and of provoking particular responses.

For example, people in intimate relationships know how to make each other angry or hostile; they know what to do to create frustration; they can identify specific behaviors in their partners that will create depression or pessimism in themselves; and they can generally describe scenarios that make them (and/or their partners) feel helpless and out of control.

In essence, then, your partner *knows* how to hurt you, and you, in turn, know how to hurt your partner back, although neither of your actions may always be conscious. You also both may know how to stop your unhealthy behavior. But all too often you find yourself behaving in ways that are counterproductive and even self-sabotaging.

Understanding these rudiments of psychology will give you a new perspective on how you and your partner behave in your problematic relationship. Once you can consciously describe even a few steps of your dangerous dance, you will be in a far better position to plan an effective attack on the toxic patterns that need to be changed.

The guiding principle of behavior modification is this: To stop a dangerous behavior, remove the reinforcement; to replace the dangerous behavior with a healthier one, identify the new action and provide a continuous reinforcement for it.

Before we proceed to the cures, we need to explore how psychological poisons become embedded in relationships.

6

The Hostile Heart

Linda is standing in her bedroom, suddenly ashamed, struck by the absurdity of her behavior. She is actually smelling one of Peter's T-shirts, testing for the scent of his perspiration, looking for evidence that he really was playing basketball with the guys after work, as he had said. Her suspicion was aroused when, after arriving home nearly two hours late, he looked remarkably unexerted and notably unperspired, despite his story of an "exhausting but really fun game." She was, in fact, looking for proof that he was lying.

What am I doing? Linda asks herself incredulously. She had never been particularly jealous, even in light of Peter's previous affairs, and she had never before engaged in such surreptitious and, to her mind, "low class" behavior.

This is getting really sick, Linda thinks, sighing. She is embarrassed by her action.

Not only has Linda become distrustful and suspicious of Peter's every move, but she has displayed noticeable changes in her attitudes toward people in general, both men and women. Yesterday, at lunch, she spent nearly half the time only vaguely listening to her friend, concentrating instead on other women in the restaurant and wondering which ones were cheating with other women's husbands. Then, driving home, she found herself inspecting men in cars at stoplights, pondering the possibilities that they too were running around on their wives.

I'm becoming such a miserable cynic, Linda thinks. *I don't believe there's a loyal husband alive. I was never this kind of a person. I just can't stand what this whole thing is doing to me.*

Cardiac Poisoning by Cynicism, Jealousy, Distrust, and Negativity

Linda realizes how her personality is changing for the worse while she tries to wait out Peter's affair in silence. What she probably does not recognize is the damage she may be causing her heart and cardiovascular system in the process. Linda is riddled with feelings of cynicism, negativity, distrust, and jealousy—emotions that are known to produce cardiac poisons. In short, Linda is developing a hostile heart.

The distrust, jealousy, and cynicism are manifesting themselves in several ways. Sometimes Linda is quiet, withdrawn, and depressed when she is around Peter, wholly uninterested and unresponsive to his sexual overtures, which she construes to be the result only of his guilt. At other times she makes snide, biting comments that contaminate the emotional climate in their home. She displays her suspiciousness and distrust by closely questioning Peter as to his whereabouts and, as she says, "watching him squirm." But her anger remains shrouded in cynicism and depression; she never confronts the issue of Peter's infidelity directly.

Ironically, Linda's behavior provides the perfect rationalization to Peter for his indiscretions. In his self-defense, Peter pleads that, since Linda withholds sex, "what's a guy to do?" Furthermore, he rationalizes, "If she's going to be so damn depressed and *depressing,*" it's at least understandable—even if unacceptable—that he seek more upbeat companionship outside the marriage. Besides, he continues, since she is so "paranoid" and suspicious of his every move, he might as well sleep with another woman since Linda would accuse him even if he didn't. So, to bolster his rationalizations and justify his unfaithfulness, Peter develops a sense of righteous resentment and hostility toward his wife. Moreover, he even convinces himself that Linda is cheating on him.

Now and again he does feel a pang of conscience. But, for the most part, he conveniently turns a blind eye to the fact that it is *his* unfaithful behavior that has engendered Linda's depression and suspiciousness. Linda's coldness and thinly veiled hostility toward him breeds a form of cynicism in Peter. Infidelity becomes "understandable" in his distorted moral calculus. According to his cynical outlook, "real" men fool around on their wives sooner or later anyway. By virtue of his own cynicism, resentment, and negativity, Peter too is developing a hostile heart.

Linda's cynicism and distrust have created their mirror image in Peter through a process called psychological *projection*. Projection is a defense mechanism through which an individual protects himself from painful self-confrontation by seeing his own faults or impulses in other people. He *projects* onto others what actually exists within himself.

More Cardiac Poisoning by Domination and Control

In addition to cynicism and negativity, the need to dominate other people and to be in total control of all situations is harmful to the cardiovascular system. Furthermore, the victims of control by another are imperiled as well. Feeling continually manipulated or exploited generates the toxic emotions of frustration and hostility. Dan and his overbearing boss, Hank, are a case in point.

By disposition, Hank has an excessive need to control other people and all situations. According to Dan, Hank's need to control others and to continually demonstrate his dominant position gradually has become exaggerated over the twenty-five years of their association. In part, the dramatic growth of Hank's business and, correspondingly, the increase in how much seems to be "on the line" when decisions involve money, employees, or public perception explain Hank's strong need to stay on top of everybody and everything. The higher the stakes, the greater Hank's feelings of anxiety and stress become, thereby stimulating an even greater need to remain in control.

Over the years, Hank has become what Dan calls a "control freak." Dan recalls the countless instances when Hank abused his authority by demanding that Dan forgo social plans or family obligations in order to report to the office for an "emergency" meeting. More often than not, the so-called emergencies were just routine issues that could easily have been addressed on the next business day. Or, they turned out to be another family crisis that Dan was required to manage but over which he could exercise no control without Hank's consent.

Hank uses every opportunity to undermine Dan's legitimate authority in areas that fall squarely within Dan's executive domain. Again, Dan describes numerous infuriating times when his business strategies or delegated tasks were sabotaged by Hank's contravening orders. In such instances, Hank would call an employee into his office and arbitrarily override Dan's directives. Since Hank generally failed to inform him of such changes, Dan would have to learn of them from his own staff. This caused him not only embarrassment at being unable to manage his department, but a humiliating sense of impotence since he feared openly confronting Hank on the issue.

To keep his upper hand psychologically, Hank demonstrates remarkable manipulative skills. He verbally degrades Dan, often at executive committee or board meetings as well as in private. Moreover, since he is an acute human observer and a person of considerable intellect, there is always just enough truth in Hank's remarks and put-downs to disarm Dan completely, leaving him at a loss both for words and for self-esteem.

Despite his passive acquiescence to Hank's control, Dan seethes internally. He hates the fact that his expensive lifestyle (which Dan's wife shows no willingness to downgrade) is predicated on an income that he must earn by silently enduring the exploitation, manipulation, and stress of Hank's overcontrolling personality.

Like many others who have been oppressed, Dan utilizes his family to become, in turn, the oppressor. In a displacement of his hostility and frustration, Dan treats his wife and son just as Hank treats him—from excessive arbitrary displays of control and dominance to unbridled criticism and attacks on their self-esteem.

A person, such as Hank, who needs to be in control of everybody and everything is not the only one at risk. Clearly, the "object" or "victim" of that control—in this case, Dan—is at least equally endangered. Not only does the oppressed party run the risk of replicating the oppressor's excessive control in other situations, but he or she must suffer the indignities of psychological subjugation. It is maddening to have another person disenfranchise you of your rights as an adult to act autonomously and even to make your own mistakes.

If an individual continually tries to prevent you from acting as an independent adult, intense feelings of resentment, frustration, and hostility will result. Moreover, when that other person strips away your control—or infringes on it in significant ways—you will, to varying degrees, feel perilously out of control. By virtue of being exploited and manipulated, then, helplessness is engendered and your physical and mental health are consequently endangered.

The Damage of Excessive Control

Take the case of Nancy and Sam. Thirteen years ago, while Nancy was in her mid-thirties and divorcing her first husband, she met Sam, a successful corporate attorney. Sam seemed a real "take charge" kind of guy, just the type of person she needed and wanted in her life. She was worn out from trying to manage everything on her own.

The breakup of Nancy's marriage had left her feeling alone, frightened, and stressed. When Sam offered to help, Nancy was more than willing to allow him to make virtually all of her decisions. Sam found and leased her an apartment. He reviewed all the legal documents pertaining to her divorce, advising her every step of the way, much to the consternation of her own attorney. Sam even changed her "look," buying Nancy a whole new wardrobe complete with expensive jewelry, since he felt that she didn't have clothes suitable for the companion of a man of *his* status.

When Sam and Nancy married, the balance of control was entirely one-sided and remained so throughout the first seven years of their marriage. Gradually, Nancy, now in her early forties, had become increasingly dissatisfied with her complete lack of responsibility and autonomy. She tried to rationalize (with Sam's strong influence) that, since he was the only one who earned money, he was entitled to have total control in their relationship.

But Sam wielded that control with a heavy hand. He required Nancy to produce receipts for all money spent, no matter how small or incidental the sum. When they had a baby, he insisted on calling all the shots regarding the domestic help they hired, how much time Nancy was "allowed" to spend away from the baby and home, when and where they went on family outings, and with whom they associated in social engagements as a couple.

Originally, Sam and Nancy both subscribed to the traditional model of marriage: The husband earns the money and "wears the pants" regarding all major decisions; the wife is a homemaker, willing to subjugate all her decisions to his. However, Sam's need to be in control of *everything*—his wife, their child, their domestic help, and *all* expenditures—exceeded even the most traditional models of marriage. The explicit rule of the house was that Nancy was *never* to challenge Sam's authority or even to disagree with him. It was an oppressive environment.

Sam not only tried to maintain total control but became mercilessly critical. On the rare occasions when Nancy failed to follow his instructions exactly, or if she made any kind of error, he berated her for "not paying attention," "being careless," or "not living up to her obligations."

By the time Nancy came to see me, she was quite depressed. As the control structure of her marriage was revealed in therapy, Nancy explained that she thought her situation was common in households of nonworking women and, by inference, believed that she was "just having a bit of trouble handling things," a perception completely confirmed by Sam. As we began discussing how Sam's excessive need to control her (and everyone else in his life) was not only inappropriate but harmful to her health as well as to Sam's, Nancy's unexpressed rage began to surface. She realized the extent of her collusion in creating the current state of affairs—by initially rewarding Sam for assuming complete responsibility for her life and thereafter passively submitting to the status quo.

Nancy's decision to seek therapy (which was really Sam's decision—he even "found" and selected me) initially seemed to exacerbate the problems. Sam used the fact that Nancy was "depressed enough to see a psychologist" and therefore "not mentally well" to bolster his role as total controller. Sadly, Nancy deferred to Sam's "superior intelligence and judgment," agreeing that she was too troubled to effectively manage any part of her life.

By nature and background, Nancy was highly unassertive and suffered from low self-esteem. Early in therapy, she felt unable and entirely unwilling to confront Sam in order to assert her rights as an adult. As a result, her frustration and resentment intensified and her depression deepened.

Nancy was enraged with Sam for reducing her to the psychological level of a helpless child. Since she couldn't or wouldn't express her anger openly, she acted it out in passive-aggressive ways that only ignited his already overly hostile personality.

For example, she shut down entirely on Sam sexually. What she did with her body was the last vestige of control that Nancy felt she held. She spent money extravagantly, even beyond their substantial means, and began "losing" the receipts and "forgetting" to enter checks. Nancy's actions, coupled with Sam's sexual frustration, intensified his anger, thereby raising the ante in what had become a vicious struggle for control and domination.

The case of Nancy and Sam shows clearly how both partners in a toxic relationship are affected negatively by one's exercise of excessive, unrealistic, and unwarranted control over the other. In addition to her clinical depression, Nancy suffered from migraine headaches, high blood pressure, recurrent colds and flus, plus two frightening, irregular Pap smears within eighteen months, which necessitated an outpatient surgical procedure to prevent the possible development of cancer.

Sam's doctor declared him a "walking time bomb." With a cholesterol count over 300, high blood pressure, and thirty-five pounds of extra girth, the doctor warned Sam that he was primed for a heart attack. Of course, Sam's risk was multiplied by his overcontrolling, hostile Type A personality.

Cardiac Poisoning by Turning Anger Against Yourself

Aggression and hatred directed toward yourself is one of the most dangerous and debilitating forms of hostility. It is likely to produce the same cardiovascular problems as those associated with anger at other people. Moreover, the attack on your self-esteem also will produce depression, negativity, and pessimism—the harbingers of immune system breakdown.

In therapy, Nancy learned that her hostile heart resulted from the intense anger that she directed against herself. In fact, depression frequently can be understood as anger turned inward. In this sense, Nancy was the captive of a protracted siege on her self-esteem.

Nancy's self-esteem was not in good shape even when she first met Sam. In large measure, that is why she distrusted her judgment and willingly yielded control to him. But, with the passage of years and Sam's unremitting criticism and insidious insults, Nancy's self-esteem bottomed out.

Inwardly directed hostility is frequently acted out against the partner as well. In Nancy's case, for example, her withholding of sex, spending money, and "forgetting" receipts were passive-aggressive acts of retaliation against Sam's excessive control.

Eventually, then, the hostile heart that harbors anger against the self also hurts the partner. In fact, chronic hostility, regardless of the reason, produces a self-perpetuating chain reaction of anger, which is the subject of the next chapter.

7

Chains of Anger

To handle anger in an intimate relationship is a tricky matter.

On one hand, failing to express any anger or other negative feelings—sometimes called emotional suppression—is a known correlate of cancer. On the other hand, anger that is too frequently aroused and expressed—especially in destructive ways—threatens the viability of the relationship and also endangers the physical and emotional health of the partners.

It is virtually inconceivable for two healthy, autonomous adults to be in an intimate relationship and *not* to experience anger with each other periodically. Inevitably, intimacy and interdependence involve stepping on your partner's toes once in a while.

The couple who avoids conflict altogether, in fact, exhibits a worrisome lack of trust since one or both partners must fear that an open outbreak of hostility might rupture the relationship irreparably. Moreover, partners who avoid conflict not only run a health risk from emotional suppression, but they fail to solidify their intimacy since an occasional constructive argument often yields information that is crucial to effective problem solving.

Helpful Versus Harmful Fighting

The fact that a couple engages in periodic conflicts, arguments, and expressions of anger—provided that no physical violence is involved—does not indicate that their relationship is troubled. In fact, what distinguishes healthy, functional couples from those who are dysfunctional is not the absence of conflicts but rather the *form* the conflicts take. Functional couples fight in ways that are *constructive* to the long-term maintenance of the relationship; dysfunctional couples engage in *destructive* conflicts that erode the fabric of their bond.

During *constructive conflict*, there is an increase in the amount of information exchanged. No questions or doubts are raised as to the basic stability, durability, or love in the relationship. Both partners display a willingness to work through and resolve the conflict so that they better understand each other and so that future conflicts over the same or similar issues can be prevented. Finally, the tactics of constructive conflict are open, flexible, friendly, and noncoercive.

By contrast, during *destructive conflict*, the amount of information exchanged is decreased due to negative communication tactics such as the "silent treatment" or the "I don't want to discuss it" approach. Questions and doubts are raised concerning the stability, durability, and love in the relationship. For example, in a marital conflict, divorce or separation may be mentioned, proposed, or threatened. At least one partner fails to display a willingness to work through the issues that lie behind the anger or conflict, thereby cutting off the process before any resolution can be reached. As a consequence, recurrent fights over the same or similar issues occur. Finally, tactics of threat, coercion, verbal attack, and insult are used, and/or actual physical violence may take place.

A workable litmus test for whether you are handling conflict constructively or destructively is simply to ask yourself whether you fight repeatedly about the *same* issues. If you do, your conflicts probably are destructive, since no resolution has been reached. On the other hand, if you confidently can say that you do *not* have the same arguments repeatedly, your mode of conflict is more likely to be constructive.

Destructive conflict generally produces *chains of anger*—cycles of mutual provocation and response that eventually can ignite frightening explosions of hostility. Hurtful verbal assaults typically are associated with the eruption of anger, which then sets the stage for the next display of aggression. With some couples, the repetitive cycle of destructive conflict becomes so exhausting and draining that either mutual or one-sided conflict avoidance develops. This further undermines the basis of intimacy by diminishing constructive communication and blocking self-disclosure.

Once a relationship is troubled by pervasive hostility—either openly expressed or covertly experienced—it is difficult for either member to objectively see the cause or the cure of the problem. Hostility disrupts your ability to think and behave rationally because it creates defensiveness. When your psychological armor is on, it's very hard to see clearly through the visor.

By gaining insight into the causes of other couples' chains of anger, you may be able to see some of your problems less defensively.

"At Least Get Angry and Prove You Still Care"

Bob prides himself on his newly found self-discipline. At 52, he awakens every morning by six o'clock, does a series of push-ups and sit-ups before eating his low-cholesterol, low-fat, low-calorie breakfast, and then runs five miles. He leaves work by five o'clock every afternoon so that he can spend another couple of hours at the gym. On weekends, he allows himself to sleep until seven o'clock, follows his usual dietary and exercise regimen, and plays several sets of competitive tennis with friends in the afternoon. He has followed his regimen faithfully now for ten months.

Everyone tells Bob that he looks great, but Bob doesn't feel well emotionally. Much of the time he is very anxious. Even more often, he senses a deep depression with which he can't quite connect. The most aggravating thing is that, with all his exercise and dietary discipline, his doctor remains concerned about Bob's "borderline high" cholesterol and blood pressure.

What Bob doesn't realize is that in recent months, his health concerns have become more obsessions than pleasures and have made him almost entirely self-focused. He has withdrawn both emotionally and sexually from Fran, his wife of twenty-five years. Bob doesn't completely understand the reasons for his withdrawal, except that by the time he is finished with his rigorous exercises he has little energy left for her.

The truth is that Bob isn't particularly concerned about his marriage. He believes that his exercise and diet programs are more important and that eventually Fran will "come around" and understand.

Fran, on the other hand, is deeply upset and angry about Bob's behavior. Thus far, she shows no signs of accepting the "new Bob" and makes no secret of her unhappiness.

One Saturday, Bob returns from his morning jog to Fran's now familiar aura of anger. Ostensibly cleaning the kitchen, she slams down a pot, throws the dishrag in the sink, and finally turns to Bob.

"Now, I suppose you don't have enough energy left even to talk to me. What about the walks we used to take together? Then we could talk to each other. And I guess you're off this afternoon for your almighty tennis game again?"

"Really, Fran," Bob replies, "I don't want to get into this. You know jogging is better for me than a stroll. I can't see why you should be so angry when all I'm trying to do is watch out for my health. I'd think if you really loved me, you'd be more supportive."

This line of defense infuriates Fran further. "I'd think that if *you* really loved *me*, you'd want to spend at least *some* of your time with me. Maybe even touch me once in a while . . . or is sex with an old lady not enough exercise for you?"

"Oh, Fran," Bob sighs as he walks out of the room, "leave it alone . . . and get off my back."

Fran sits down at the kitchen table, head in hands, and cries softly. She berates herself for losing her temper again, but she feels so lonely and frustrated. Nothing she says or does seems to get any kind of reaction from him. *If he'd just yell at me or get really angry, at least I'd know that he still cared,* she thinks.

That evening, Bob and Fran go out with two other couples. As usual, Bob is his charming, outgoing self and Fran is pleasant and appropriate. But the moment they get in the car to drive home, Bob shuts down.

"Why don't you talk to me when we're alone?" Fran asks plaintively. "You talk to everyone else but with me you just clam up."

"What do you want from me?" Bob asks quietly. "I go out with your friends—people I don't even like—and make an effort to be sociable. Now you're angry with me for being nice to them. I can't win for losing." They drive home in silence.

Later, Fran lies in bed with one eye on the television and one on Bob, who is doing his thirty-minute nighttime workout on the treadmill.

"No wonder we never make love anymore," Fran snaps. "You expend every bit of energy on your stupid workouts. Or maybe you're getting sex from someone else."

"Look, Fran," Bob responds. "I'm not going to let my blood pressure go out of control by allowing you to get my goat. If you want a fight, you can fight with yourself. I'm going to sleep."

With each passing day, the chain of anger between Fran and Bob continues to grow, with the same arguments, the festering frustration and hostility, and the failure of both to control their actions long enough to get to the bottom of their troubles.

When Fran and Bob finally came to therapy, they were on the verge of separating. She couldn't take the rejection and isolation anymore, and he couldn't take the criticism and hostility. They had become adept at pushing each other's buttons and at reinforcing each other's negative behavior.

The more Bob focused his attention and energy on his compulsive exercise and health pursuits, the less time and energy he had for Fran. Of course, his withdrawal and preoccupation only further inflamed her hurt and anger. In turn, Fran's verbal attacks became more pointed and ultimately cruel. She could find no other way of handling her profound sense of rejection and alienation from the husband she still loved. With Bob's increasing withdrawal, she became obsessed with the notion of regaining their emotional connection, if not through affection then through anger.

However, Fran's hostility served only to reinforce Bob's avoidance behavior. He rationalized that getting "pulled into an argument" would only hurt his health. Moreover, he attributed his lack of sexual interest to her aggressiveness, which completely "turned him off."

In therapy, Bob and Fran eventually were able to break the destructive cycle that had all but destroyed a long and, until fairly recently, happy marriage. In time, Bob understood that his obsessive health concerns were a defensive way of coping with dying. Bob's father and grandfather had died in their mid-fifties from heart conditions; his father had actually died during sexual intercourse with Bob's mother. And Bob's major recollection of his parents' marriage was of their screaming fights driven by his mother's provocations and his father's fiery temper.

With Bob's disclosures and realizations, Fran was able to drop some of her defensiveness and to avoid personalizing his behavior.

"So this hasn't just been about your turning off to me," she mused aloud during a particularly important session. "You've been trying to keep from dying. And I've been so hurt and angry, feeling so old, unattractive, and useless to you, that I haven't been much help."

Bob acknowledged that his sexual rejection of Fran was

linked to the painful memory of his father dying in bed with his mother.

"I need to realize that I don't have my father's heart condition or his temper. I don't need to be afraid of sex. . . . I even asked the doctor." Then, turning to his wife, he said quietly, "But it's hard, Fran. I'll need your support and understanding to get past these fears."

Bob and Fran also developed new skills for better managing conflict. I explained to Bob that the anger he was suppressing by avoiding direct confrontation with his wife was probably causing more long-term damage to his health than whatever short-term effects a brief but more open display of anger would involve. By learning the rules of constructive conflict, Bob and Fran were able to negotiate agreements about balancing time spent together with time spent alone.

They also realized that for many years, the presence at home of their three children had helped them keep their anger under wraps, since they concurred that children should not be exposed to parental fighting. After their children had grown and left home, Bob and Fran had felt strangely exposed, vulnerable to an explosion of anger and unable to invoke the rule of protecting the children as a way of controlling themselves. So, Bob had withdrawn and refused to fight, while Fran had openly seethed, becoming more and more critical and antagonistic.

Bob and Fran's story demonstrates that even long-standing relationships that have had years of relative quiescence can become infected with cycles of hostility. Their case also dramatically highlights how individuals' deep-rooted, private fears—his of dying prematurely, hers of growing old, unattractive, and "invisible"—can set off behaviors that then take on new meaning in the context of a relationship.

Bob and Fran's story is a stark reminder of how important it is to monitor your relationship as closely as you monitor your cholesterol, blood pressure, and exercise habits in the quest for good health.

"And Remember When You Said . . . ?"

Diane and Richard had been married for two years when she came to see me on the referral of her doctor. At 32, Diane had been diagnosed with rheumatoid arthritis and had undergone two knee operations due to the disease.

Because of her illness she was on full disability from work. The limitations of her illness made her unable to do many of the regular household chores that she wanted to do. So, her physical impairments underscored and compounded her already profound sense of inadequacy as a wife and a woman. To further complicate matters, her loss of income had produced greater stress on Richard, who now was hard-pressed to cover not only the couple's regular overhead but that portion of Diane's very high medical bills not covered by her insurance.

Early in our sessions, I suggested to Diane that she think of flare-ups of rheumatoid arthritis as episodes during which her immune system became so overreactive that it turned on itself and literally attacked her joints. Often, I explained, the personalities of people with this disease show an overreactive, emotional parallel as reflected in anxiety, severe frustration, stress, and explosive anger.

Diane immediately identified with this notion and proceeded to describe the emotional strains in her marriage. Almost at once, it became clear that she was sitting on a volcano of hostility—precariously contained—toward not only Richard but her family and friends. Since her rage was subject to periodic outbreaks, she was further plagued by feelings of guilt and disappointment with herself for "being so nasty with people I love who care about me."

Since her pain and frustration levels were so elevated, Diane's anger could be triggered by a myriad of events, ranging from minor to significant, and particularly by almost anything that Richard did or said that was even slightly critical.

Unfortunately, on several occasions in the past, when Diane's rage had surfaced it had been explosively ignited by the high dosages of steroids that were prescribed to treat her arthritis. At relatively high levels, steroids can sometimes create dramatic mood changes including hyperirritability and extreme agitation. Diane admitted that during these angry episodes she had said things to Richard that "were way out of line, cruel, and awful." She feared that he would not be able to forget or forgive her remarks.

Since marital therapy was clearly indicated, Richard joined the sessions. What was revealed was a chain of anger between the two that stretched back a long way, predating not only Diane's illness but their marriage. In fact, during the five years that the couple had gone together before getting married, the last three, they agreed, had been marked by constant bickering and several intense fights.

The subjects of those arguments ran the gamut from relatively minor issues, such as where to go on a particular evening or Diane's chronic lateness for dates, to graver matters, principally involving jealousy, suspiciousness, and accusations of infidelity.

Apparently, Richard had decided to propose to Diane in an attempt to stop the arguments. Although his proposal was accepted, the betrothal did little to interrupt their stormy cycle of fighting or to break the chains of hostility growing between them.

Diane and Richard lacked the necessary skills for constructive conflict resolution. None of their issues was ever settled, either before or after the marriage. Both had remarkably long memories and had stored up each point of resentment only to reintroduce it during a subsequent argument, sometimes years later. Consequently, when Diane and Richard fought, the conflict invariably returned to one or more previous unresolved grievances. Predictably, mention of the "old fight" elicited a defensive, angry response that, in turn, obscured their abilities to focus on the current argument and to reach a resolution.

Finally, of course, the couple was under a great deal of understandable stress with which neither Diane nor Richard coped well. Diane felt enormous frustration and anger about the "unfairness" of her illness and the pain, incapacitation, and disfigurement she experienced. Richard felt that he was now "married to the arthritis instead of to Diane" and simultaneously inadequate because of his inability to cure her problems. During a few of her steroid-induced rages, Diane even accused Richard of being the cause of her illness by "making me so angry that it made me sick." As a consequence, Richard felt deeply resentful, guilty, and depressed.

The good news about Diane and Richard was that they were candid about their issues and highly motivated to improve their relationship. However, both felt that they could not tolerate the frequent arguments and intense hostility any longer. So, after their first therapy session, they privately agreed "to avoid fighting with each other at all costs."

But their agreement went too far, specifying that the occasion of "one more fight" would mean divorce. Clearly, this approach was ill-conceived, and I immediately disabused them of following such an unrealistic and counterproductive path of conflict avoidance.

Diane and Richard didn't need to stop fighting altogether; they needed to learn to fight fairly, constructively, and effectively. Eventually the frequency and intensity of their arguments would decrease because their older issues would finally be resolved.

What was especially troubling to them was *why* they kept fighting and saying such mean things to each other when each clearly acknowledged still being in love. In therapy, Diane and Richard understood that their initial passion for each other had been channeled into lovemaking and expressions of affection and positive feelings; but, over time, that passion had become converted—or perverted—into a form of intense hostility.

In a memorable turning-point session, I interpreted to Diane and Richard the function that their hostility was serving in their relationship. That function was to protect each from feeling vulnerable to the other. After all, I explained, "if your dukes are up and you're poised to strike, it's impossible to let your emotional guard down enough to be vulnerable to your partner." This struck a responsive chord. They acknowledged that the accumulation of hurt over the years had so damaged them that they each felt too frightened to trust and become vulnerable to the other again. Anger, they could see, was their misguided mode of defense.

Diane and Richard are still working together in therapy and substantial progress has been made. They are learning better skills for conflict resolution and have developed many deeper understandings that have finally put to rest some of the old issues. They have both deliberately tried to drop their defensive guard and allow themselves to become vulnerable so that their positive passion can be rekindled. And, as their marital conflicts have decreased, Diane's arthritic flare-ups have similarly declined in incidence and intensity.

The Power Struggle

Another common pattern of anger between Lethal Lovers is the power struggle—the relationship held together by each partner's compulsive need to try to dominate and control the other.

In love relationships, the underlying dynamic behind this pattern often is ambivalence toward the opposite sex born of overcontrolling parental behavior by the opposite-sex parent. Thus, the man who had a dominating but nevertheless loving mother might find himself drawn to a woman whom he perceives is strong like his mother. Simultaneously, however, he is frightened by her controlling nature, which he fears will rob him of his independence.

The woman's family dynamic is similar. Typically, she has had a loving but controlling father. She likely has witnessed her mother's passive acquiescence to her father's domination, and has neither approved of nor respected her mother's subservience.

As an adult, such a woman also might find herself attracted to a man like her father. Furthermore, she might even unconsciously select a fellow who, like her, has the need to struggle against a partner's strength precisely because he fears a loss of his independence. So, like the man, this kind of woman would be simultaneously drawn and resistant to a controlling man. She desires his strength but fears becoming a passive, subservient, dependent woman like her mother.

These were the family backgrounds of Ben and Christie, who, when they first met, were attracted to each other like magnets. But, once they got together, they began alternating between periods of intense attraction and equally intense repulsion and hostility. Ben and Christie were locked in a power struggle that rapidly became dangerous to their health.

At age 40, Christie saw Ben as her last hope for being a mother. Ben, a few years her junior, also wanted children and, mostly for that reason, proposed marriage very shortly after they met. Still in the throes of romantic infatuation, Christie jumped at the opportunity for marriage and motherhood with a man who was "strong enough" to be her intellectual and personality match. But when they moved in together, big trouble started.

At first their arguments were primarily territorial: They disagreed about almost everything—whose furniture would be used in which room, how the furniture should be arranged, who would sleep on which side of the bed, and which cabinets would be used by whom in the bathroom. Even these early arguments rapidly escalated to more serious struggles concerning general control and dominance in the relationship.

Soon the power struggle began to center around two of the most difficult and explosive issues in a love relationship: money and sex. They fought about who should pay for what, how money should be managed after marriage, and whether the person making more money (in this case, Ben) should have a greater say in when and how the money should be spent. Again, they disagreed on everything, and, as with the territorial disputes, neither would relent.

Inevitably the power struggle spread to the bedroom. They fought about when to have sex, how often, what positions to use, who should be the initiator, and what kind of foreplay was best. Although their lovemaking was passionate after they argued, their sexual relationship deteriorated into yet another arena in which to struggle against each other for control.

Christie accused Ben of being flirtatious with other women. Although he adamantly denied the behavior, he proceeded to flirt flagrantly in front of Christie at the next party they attended together. Ben told Christie that he was concerned about the weight she was gaining. She responded by eating ice cream out of a gallon container in his presence, daring him to criticize her. Ben responded by shutting down sexually until she lost ten pounds.

Each railed against any attempt to be controlled by the other, and did so in ways that were perceived by the other to be controlling. And, despite the fact that Ben and Christie were both highly intelligent, neither had much insight into the sources of their problems.

The intriguing question, of course, is why Ben and Christie stayed together in what became a draining, exhausting, and enormously stressful relationship. When queried on this point in therapy, they agreed that "when we do get along, it's great." But neither seemed able to break the cycle of anger. They were each highly skilled at quickly provoking the other's hostility, although neither could understand or control the compulsion to continue fighting. Despite several deliberate attempts, they were unable to withstand a period of even one week without at least one major battle and several minor skirmishes.

Theirs was a classic power-struggle relationship. Each was so intent on watching the other's moves in order to stay protected that their own contributions to the problems went undetected. Neither Christie nor Ben understood that their defensive reactions to what each perceived as the other's control attempts were, in fact, interpreted by their partner as offensive moves designed to manipulate, exploit, and dominate. Thus, the destructive power struggle with its attendant stress and requirement for constant vigilance was perpetuated.

Because each believed their independence was threatened, neither found it possible to let down their guard and relax. Their sex life all but disappeared as a result of the tension, and their tempers shortened. Christie fell prey to one virus after another, enduring colds, flus, and bouts of irritating mouth sores. Ben began having tension headaches, shortness of breath, and chest pains.

By the time Christie came to see me, the couple had ended the relationship and Ben was involved with another woman. Sadly, the stress of Christie's ordeal with Ben probably contributed to an acute exacerbation of her endometriosis, a problem that had been relatively dormant since her late twenties, and one that cast considerable doubt on whether she would be able to become pregnant.

"Every relationship I've ever had with a man has turned sour just like this one," Christie reflected. "I'm so afraid of losing myself to a controlling man that I do totally self-destructive things just to keep my independence. But I'm bored with weak men. I have to admit, this relationship with Ben was the most difficult one yet. I really wanted to make it work, but it just tore me apart—physically and emotionally."

Breaking the Chains of Anger

These case studies are just a few examples of the complex chains of anger that develop when hostile feelings are mishandled. Of course, such chains are not restricted to intimate love relationships. They are commonly seen in parent-child interactions and in work relationships as well.

What can be done to break a destructive chain of anger? First, it is helpful to understand the psychological factors behind the problem. As in the cases of Ben and Christie, and Bob and Fran, the root of hostility often lies in the internal psychological dynamics (e.g., family backgrounds, inner fears and conflicts) of the individuals. At other times, though, the angry interaction is bred primarily by negative conditioning in the relationship itself. Such was the case with Diane and Richard.

Whatever the cause, however, the solution lies in *changing behavior*. Chains or cycles of anger are perpetuated because they are continually reinforced. The reinforcement comes in part from the predictability that hostile cycles establish. In a perverse sense, it is reassuring to know that your partner will react with hostility given a particularly provocative action on your part. While you may not like or enjoy it consciously, the chain of anger is a predictable and therefore largely controllable sequence that, in its own way, becomes a familiar and strangely comforting pattern.

Breaking such an ingrained and entrenched pattern depends on at least one partner's ability to produce an unexpected response. When I work with couples in therapy who seem trapped in their cycles of anger, I encourage them to talk calmly about what they are feeling instead of acting out their reaction in the habitual way. For example, Diane was taught to describe to Richard her feelings of frustration and pain about her illness rather than to lose her temper and yell at him over some minor infraction. On his part, Richard was encouraged to talk about his sense of impotence with respect to making her illness better and the anger it engendered.

Similarly, Fran and Bob learned to talk directly about the inner fears that plagued them and to describe how the other's behavior was making them feel instead of reactively blaming and fighting.

Calm verbalization of feelings instead of the habitual anger reaction is effective for two reasons: First, the different behavior of talking about your feelings breaks the ingrained cycle. Therefore, it is less likely to elicit the next hostile reaction in the sequenced chain of anger. Second, talking calmly about your problem permits you and your partner to develop alternative behaviors designed to counteract your hostile responses.

Chains of anger essentially are bad relationship habits. However, while overt hostility and chronic destructive conflict are highly toxic, unexpressed anger and suppressed negative feelings are silent killers, as we shall see in the next chapter.

8

Swallowing Toxic Feelings

For the fourth time, Louise and Robert have broken off their relationship. Once again, Louise had broached the subject of marriage with Robert, using what she felt was considerable tact, even delicacy. Nevertheless, Robert balked. Exploding with anger, he again demanded his "space."

"You're constantly pressuring me," he protested, "instead of giving me a chance to arrive at this decision on my own."

"If I waited for you, I'd be a sixty-year-old spinster," Louise shot back.

The argument escalated, although Louise took care to keep her temper in check. Robert accused her of being "desperate"; Louise dubbed him "a chicken." They jointly decided to "break up for good," ceasing all contact with each other until sometime in the nebulous future when they might resume a friendship.

Now, two weeks after the breakup, Louise feels lonely and depressed. Alone in her apartment, she is attempting to numb her pain with a two-pound bag of chocolate-chip cookies. In the last ten days she has gained five pounds, as she obsesses on her dilemma with Robert and compulsively overeats. Louise is particularly frustrated because she has not been able to express accurately the degree of her raging resentment toward Robert.

Impulsively she picks up the telephone receiver and begins to dial his number. Then, however, self-control prevails and she calls her best friend, Margaret, instead.

"I'm so damned angry," Louise tells Margaret. "I want to call him so I can just yell and scream. Somehow, he should pay for all the time he wasted in my life by misleading me and making me think that we'd eventually get married. Now, another six months on my biological clock has gone ticking by and I'm not one step closer to having a baby. I'm incredibly depressed."

"Look, Louise," Margaret replies, "calling Robert just to vent your anger is totally counterproductive. I'm not the only one who thinks this. Susan, Amy, and Fanny all agree. If you want to get him back, the best strategy is to act totally nonchalant— as if you really don't care so much. If you see him at the gym, be civil but distant; just don't call him or contact him in any way. If he thinks you've stopped caring, he'll come running back. And when you do get back together, don't say a word about getting married. If you keep him wondering about your feelings, he'll come around and propose."

Since Louise knows that her way hasn't worked in the past, she submits to the counsel of her well-meaning friends. Male-female strategic planning, according to her advisory group, dictates that Louise supress her anger, as well as her needs, and present herself as cool, calm, and collected. "Never let a man know he has that much control," they warn.

So Louise sits tight and leaves Robert to his "space." Doing so takes all the self-control she can muster and more patience than she ever thought she possessed. But, despite whatever strategic advantage the control might gain her, the inability to express what she feels to Robert is exacting a huge toll on her both physically and psychologically.

Louise is crippled with tension; she cries herself to sleep; and she is so depressed and anxious at work that her concentration is seriously impaired. Her supervisor already has admonished her about the decline in her job performance.

She has dated other men, but with little enthusiasm. She even had sex with one of them on their second date, just to quell the loneliness and have someone hold her. But the man never called her again, deepening her burgeoning sense of worthlessness.

Eventually, just as Louise's advisory council predicted, Robert calls. True to form, he has become intensely jealous and longs for a reconciliation with Louise. Although she is secretly thrilled by his call, Louise remains reserved, expressing neither her anger nor any terms upon which a reconciliation might be conditioned. She says nothing about her true feelings and merely agrees to see him again.

So, once again, Robert and Louise resume their relationship, with only vague promises from him about a future commitment. But, as time goes by, Louise's negative emotions—frustration, anger, loss of self-esteem—rear up again, although she makes every effort to keep them suppressed. For five months, Louise sits on her toxic feelings. Robert is amorous, but the subject of marriage remains unmentioned.

The cost of her emotional suppression eventually catches up with Louise. The problems begin with severe tension headaches, then progress to stomach irritation and pain. Her doctor suggests that she might have an incipient ulcer. She feels chronically exhausted and displays other symptoms that lead a specialist to diagnose chronic fatigue syndrome.

On the way home from the specialist's office, Louise mutters to herself, "I *am* tired; I'm sick and tired of keeping my feelings and needs hidden and acting like everything is okay with Robert when it's just not. I *do* want more from this relationship and I'm afraid to say so. With no commitments, I wonder if he'll even stick around now that I'm ill."

Louise has swallowed her anger, depression, resentment,

hurt, and frustration—psychological poisons that have damaged both her physical and emotional health.

Dan's intercom buzzes. He grimaces in anticipation of the summons conveyed by Hank's secretary.

"Dan, the boss wants to see you . . . *immediately*. Oh, and, Dan, he's on the warpath again," the secretary cautions.

Great, Dan thinks as he hustles down the long hallway to Hank's executive office. *This is just what I need on a Friday . . . enough aggravation to last for a weekend.*

Hank, clearly in a bad humor, has just returned from meeting with his accountants. Although the financial malaise of the company does not fall within Dan's realm of responsibility, Hank decides to call him on the carpet anyway.

"I think you've been too distracted by outside concerns for the company's good," Hank begins. "I get the definite impression that you've been having marital problems. Your mind just hasn't been on business, and, as a result, we're showing a loss for the last two quarters. Dan, I want to be an understanding friend, but business must come first."

Dan attempts to respond but is immediately cut off by Hank's developing diatribe. "I'm really not interested in any of your excuses. Either your concentration is one hunded percent on business or it's not, and yours emphatically is *not*. What do you plan to do about it?"

Dan feels the familiar frustration and anger welling up inside. The reason his mind hasn't been all on business, he explains to himself, is because he spends half his time dealing with Hank's family problems.

Dan sees no possibility of expressing his feelings to Hank. He responds as he always does: He swallows his anger and frustration and tells Hank what he wants to hear.

"Okay, boss," Dan says in his typically solicitous way. "I'll try to improve my concentration. Is there anything in particular that I can do to help out with the financial problems? I know that money is outside of my bailiwick, but you just let me know what I can do."

"Pay attention to business," Hank snaps. "That's all I ask. Is it too much, considering what you're paid?"

Then Hank softens his tone and changes gears. "Dan," he says, "I need a favor. The accountants caught my daughter with her sticky hands in the till again. It seems she's been using her corporate credit card to buy stuff for herself. Look, I'd appreciate it if you'd have a little talk with her."

Hank abruptly turns his attention away from Dan, picks up the phone, and begins speaking to his secretary. He perfunctorily dismisses Dan with a wave of his hand, then covers the phone momentarily and snaps, "That's it. Get back to work. Oh, and get a handle on my daughter right away. If she doesn't stop this foolishness, I'm going to hold you responsible."

Dan leaves Hank's office furious with his boss, as usual, and disgusted with himself. *How much more of this abuse can I take?* he wonders. *This guy is completely unreasonable and irrational. If I had one shred of guts or self-respect, I'd tell him where to stick it.*

Since the hour is late, Dan packs up his briefcase and leaves the office, deciding to tackle the confrontation with Hank's daughter on Monday. On his way home, he stops at a local watering hole, unloads some of his problems on a sympathetic bartender, then drives to the liquor store to buy three fifths of vodka for the weekend.

As soon as he walks into the house, his wife greets him with a new litany of problems. "The bathroom pipe sprung a big leak and the plumber's bill was a hundred twenty dollars. And Eric skipped school again. The vice principal called. You'll have to talk to him."

"I'm not talking to anybody, including you," Dan says gruffly. He pours himself a triple vodka and settles into his armchair, with the intention of getting as drunk as possible.

Along with the vodka that Dan is swigging down, he is swallowing a bellyful of toxic feelings.

* * *

Peter calls Linda at five-thirty with what sounds like a whopper of a story. "Sorry, hon," he says tenderly, "the boss just announced an all-night meeting. There's no way I can get out of being there, and I'll be completely unreachable by phone. It's a strategic planning session for our new marketing campaign. I should be home by midnight, but don't wait up."

Linda has decided to take a kinder, gentler approach with Peter. No longer indulging her depression, she has determined to fight for her husband by being "the perfect wife." So, despite her suspicion and indignation at what she is sure is Peter's lie, she replies just as tenderly, "Okay, sweetie. Thanks for calling. I won't wait up on purpose, but I just might be awake for some loving when you finally roll in. I hope you remember to eat some dinner."

"Don't worry, babe. I'll be fine. Love and kisses."

It's all sickeningly sweet.

After a month of depression, emotional coldness, and sexual withdrawal, Linda has decided to put a lid on her negative feelings.

"If I'm going to have a fighting chance," she confides to a friend, "I have to give him some darn good reasons to stay married."

Her friend strongly objects. "Linda, from what you've told me, your husband is cheating on you. And this isn't the first time. I just can't see how you can stay silent about it, let alone be so nice and loving when you clearly don't feel that way. It's not honest!"

"You're right," Linda answers. "It's definitely not honest. But I have to hide my anger and hurt and do everything to keep them from coming to the surface. Knowing Peter, his conscience will win out and he'll give up the girl. Besides, he always gets bored with his girlfriends sooner or later."

"You know," her friend responds, "I realize that you must love him a lot to put up with this stuff. But the impression I get is that you don't love yourself—at least, you sure don't seem to respect yourself. You're a terrific woman, Linda, and you simply don't deserve to be treated this way. I think Peter needs to know how hurt and angry you feel."

The friend is a wise woman. Linda is swallowing her toxic feelings, and the psychological poisons are likely what's been eating away at her stomach and probably damaging her health in other ways as well. While she may be hiding her feelings from Peter, she is doing so only at great expense to her emotional and physical health.

Why Do People Swallow Toxic Feelings?

Louise, Dan, and Linda all could offer perfectly "logical" explanations for suppressing their negative feelings. Louise and her friends believe that to express such emotions would be a tactical error. If she expressed her anger, sense of rejection, depression, and frustration, Linda reasons, Robert's reluctance to propose marriage might be justified. After all, she asks rhetorically, who would want to hook up with such a negative woman?

For Dan, the reasons are embedded in his formal role as Hank's subordinate. Notwithstanding his senior executive status in the company, Dan knows that he simply cannot and dare not talk back to his boss. Instead, Dan swallows his negative feelings because he knows that Hank's authoritarian personality will never tolerate their expression.

Linda rationalizes that she can't express her anger and hurt for fear that Peter will leave her. Her beliefs are largely the product of her mother's instruction: A wife's job is to keep her husband happy—to feed him well, satisfy him sexually, and pump up his ego constantly. In the event that he strays (as Linda's mother believed all husbands do), the wise wife keeps her mouth shut, her hurt feelings to herself, and commits herself instead to working harder to make home and hearth a more desirable place. A devout Catholic, Linda's mother also was clear that divorce could never be an option. Therefore, Linda feels that her only alternative is to make the best of a bad situation.

Many people find it quite difficult to openly express fear, depression, anger, resentment, and other unpleasant emotions. But, when suppressed or swallowed, these emotions can become especially toxic.

Typically, when negative feelings—especially hostility and resentment—are kept in check for a length of time, they become more intense. Eventually, their intensity can take the form of repressed rage, an emotion that can feel very threatening.

People who have long-suppressed negative feelings often fear that an emotional explosion, of huge and uncontrollable proportions, might occur if the lid on their suppressed feelings suddenly was lifted. Moreover, the eruption of rage might lead to physical violence and/or verbal abuse, which could cause irreparable damage to their relationship. Thus, the fear of loss of control becomes the prevailing reason for emotional suppression. Ironically, the longer your hostility festers unexpressed, the greater the chances that you will actually lose control when your seething rage inevitably surfaces.

If your partner is extremely and overtly hostile, you may be intimidated into keeping your negative feelings suppressed. In other words, if you anticipate an irate, angrily defensive, or even physically violent response from your partner to your expression of negative feelings, you might opt instead to protect yourself by simply swallowing them. Under these circumstances, you would become conditioned by your partner into hiding your negative feelings, perhaps even from yourself.

Childhood Lessons in Dealing with Negative Feelings

Most people lack the skills to express negative feelings constructively and appropriately. You probably were taught as a child that overt displays of anger, such as temper tantrums or screaming, were wrong and unacceptable. Likely you were told that acting out your anger through physical means such as hitting or kicking also was unacceptable. But, like most people, you probably were not taught the correct or acceptable ways to express negative feelings.

Consequently, you may have learned as a child simply to lump together your negative feelings into a generalized, undifferentiated response—such as crying, sulking, or withdrawing. For these reasons, your negative feelings may seem mysterious, confusing, ill-defined, or simply unavailable to your awareness and analysis.

It follows, then, that if you cannot identify your feelings you will not be able to express yourself accurately. To further complicate matters, the inability to express yourself appropriately or, indeed, even to understand what your feelings are creates more frustration. As we have seen, frustration is the handmaiden of further hostility. Thus, the negative, vicious cycle continues.

Another consequence of what you may have learned about negative feelings as a child is that such feelings are socially unacceptable. The result, then, is that your negative feelings are suppressed because they are psychologically forbidden, presumably not befitting the character of a decent, mature adult. In truth, of course, this is not the case. There are situations in which anger, for example, is a wholly appropriate and adaptive response. If you have been deceived, betrayed, cheated, exploited, or otherwise mistreated, a degree of anger is a healthy and probably necessary reaction.

What Feelings Get Buried and Why?

The most commonly suppressed negative feelings are anxiety, anger, depression, and fear.

Men, in particular, have difficulty identifying and expressing emotions that they construe as "weak," "soft," or "unmanly." Such feelings include not only fear and anxiety but positive emotions such as vulnerability, dependency, and even love.

Many cardiac rehabilitation programs feature psychotherapy groups to help men express their fears and anxieties first to one another and, eventually, to their wives and friends. These

men also are aided in identifying hostile feelings and expressing them appropriately.

If something has made an individual angry, he is encouraged
to express his anger directly, then immediately to seek a
solution for what made him angry so as to avoid the problem
in the future.

Obviously, love, kindness, and other positive emotions are
not toxic; on the contrary, they are immensely healthy and,
indeed, even healing. So what happens when these positive
feelings are constantly suppressed or withheld? Love requires
expression—verbally and nonverbally—in order to be adequately felt and communicated so that it can be nurtured and
reciprocated. Kind feelings that are left unexpressed fail to
translate into acts of altruism or generosity toward others.
Consequently, their meaning and even their validity become
questionable. Thus, a person who constantly suppresses positive, loving feelings toward others suffers a life that is largely
bereft of love and positivity from others. In this way, then,
swallowing positive feelings certainly can become toxic as well.

Both men and women can develop health problems from
suppressing yet another category of feelings: their own needs.
Indeed, the so-called cancer personality is described as a stoic,
self-denying sort who does not express what is bothering him
or her and who therefore denies important needs.[6] This personality characteristic—the apparent inability to express one's
needs—is the most commonly cited psychological factor in the
development of the disease. Moreover, its presence is generally
predictive of an unfavorable prognosis among those patients
who have cancer.

At age 57, Sylvia is a classic "superwife-mother-sister" and all-
around martyr. With their third child in college and the older
two married, Sylvia and her husband, Frank, now live alone
for the first time in twenty-six years. Nevertheless, Sylvia is
intimately involved in her children's and grandchildren's lives

and continues to cater to their every need as she did all the years they lived at home.

Sylvia cooks every holiday meal for a crowd of at least twenty. Every Friday night, she has her family to the house for dinner; on Sundays, she has her husband's. And she refuses to allow anyone to help her. When someone offers to bring food, she replies, "Don't trouble yourself. I've got nothing better to do." So, she shops, cooks, bakes, and insists on doing all the cleaning up after the company has gone. Invariably, she is exhausted by the evening's close.

Everyone allows Sylvia to do all the work. They rationalize among themselves that, "This is the only thing that makes her happy," or, "She's so stubborn, what's the use?"

Lately, Sylvia looks more tired than usual. Much of the time she seems worried and preoccupied. But she denies having any problems and responds, "Everything's just fine," or, "I'm okay, just a little tired," when family members and friends ask after her health.

Sylvia's biggest problem is that she cannot express her needs to anyone. Indeed, at this point in her life, Sylvia isn't even sure what her needs are—except that she *needs* to take care of everyone else. The truth is that Sylvia doesn't feel that she has the right to ask anything of anyone. She is a stoic, self-denying personality.

After so many years of martyrdom, Sylvia has actually conditioned her children and husband to disregard her needs. The whole family colludes with Sylvia's suppression of her feelings. On the rare occasions when she has attempted to tell one of her kids about a problem or to express some kind of negative feeling, the typical response she receives is, "Oh, Mom, knock it off. You're not like one of those griping, unhappy women!" And Frank, who is also an emotional suppressor, discounts her feelings by saying, "Come on, honey. We're not ones to complain. Things will work out, whatever they are."

Now, Sylvia has been diagnosed with advanced colon cancer.

* * *

The stoic, self-denying personality, like Sylvia's, cannot and does not let others (or even herself) know what is needed. As a way of coping with the denial, this type of individual maintains the suppression of his or her needs by taking care of everyone else's. Inevitably, however, putting other people's needs always ahead of your own leads to resentment and frustration. And, since those negative feelings are equally unacceptable, they too are suppressed. But suppressed needs do not just disappear. They multiply inside us—metaphorically *and* actually—like life-threatening malignant cells.

What Happens When Feelings Are Not Expressed?

Psychological research and theory point to a number of serious consequences when feelings—especially negative ones—and needs are not expressed. First, people who do not express their feelings and needs are more likely to get sick, more likely to remain sick, have poor prognoses for recovering, and are more likely to die sooner than are people who express their feelings and needs adequately and appropriately.[7]

Second, unexpressed negative feelings feed on themselves, thereby compounding the psychological problems as well as the physiological consequences. Unexpressed anger, for example, can become internalized, or turned against the self, and manifested as depression or severe anxiety. Blocked negative emotions cause frustration to build, leading to greater hostility, further suppression, and more frustration.

In short, when negative feelings are swallowed, they become toxic to both body and mind. Researchers identified self-sacrifice, denial of hostility or anger, and nonexpression of emotion as the factors most related to an unfavorable prognosis in cancer patients and possibly to the susceptibility to the disease as well. These researchers also found evidence to suggest that the same personality style—emotional repression—characterizes the "immunosuppression-prone" individual who may be particularly vulnerable to AIDS.[8]

In contrast, studies that have identified some of the factors most correlated with positive prognoses among cancer patients, and with better outcomes among AIDS patients, emphasize the ability to express one's needs and emotions as key.[9]

In addition to the immune system, the cardiovascular system can be damaged by unexpressed feelings, especially in men. There is scientific evidence that men who bury negative emotions—particularly anxiety—are more likely to have dangerously high cholesterol levels.[10]

Women suffer similarly. A recent eighteen-year study shows the perilous effects for women of not expressing their anger. Researchers found a strikingly higher mortality rate for women who suppressed their anger as compared to those who expressed it.[11]

These studies and many others illustrate just how physically toxic negative emotions can become when they are swallowed instead of expressed openly and coped with appropriately. Psychiatric symptoms, as well, can result when powerful negative emotions remain inside, producing psychological poisons.

One of my patients, Joan, suffers from extreme anxiety and episodic depression. Joan is one of the nicest people I've ever met—nice to everyone, that is, except herself.

As a young child, Joan learned from her mother that it is unacceptable to get angry with people you love; she was taught by her father that girls (and, of course, women) simply *must not* express negative feelings of any kind to men. So, Joan smiled sweetly even when she felt furious. She became so adept at hiding her negative feelings in order to avoid criticism from others that she soon became unable even to acknowledge the forbidden emotions to herself.

As a woman of 45, Joan continues to find her anger the most threatening and frightening emotion of all. When her husband, daughter, or other members of her family do things that upset her, she immediately disguises the anger from herself and others by becoming severely nervous, uncontrollably tearful, or depressed. Sometimes she responds by pushing herself harder and harder to do extraordinary amounts of physical work around the house until she virtually collapses from exhaustion. The fatigue then permits her to go to bed for several days so that she can regain her composure and allow the unexpressed, unacknowledged anger to dissipate.

Since Joan cannot give herself permission to express her anger directly or, generally, even to feel it, she turns the anger against herself. Once directed at herself, the anger becomes punitive as she overworks or brutally criticizes herself until she becomes intolerably depressed. Either way, she is so weakened by her symptoms that it becomes impossible for her to behave angrily toward anybody except herself.

When Joan first came to therapy, she would not acknowledge any angry feelings. Instead, she would say only that "the problem is with my nerves" or would question why she was so "inadequate compared to other women." Over the course of our long relationship, however, she has learned to recognize raging but unexpressed hostility in the form of psychiatric symptoms. Sometimes, when she smiles while simultaneously shaking and verging on tears, I simply ask, "Who made you feel so angry?" Although she now at least can answer the question, she still puts herself through tortures of depression, fatigue, and high anxiety before she is finally ready to address the issue or person that aroused her forbidden anger.

Of course, Joan has a lot more work to do in therapy. Sadly, deeply rooted problems in her marriage perpetuate the negative cycle of repressed emotions and psychiatric illness. As a result, Joan's progress is often three steps forward and two steps back, with a great deal of frustration and self-criticism along the way.

Understanding and Using Your Symptoms as Messages

Not everyone who develops cancer, cardiovascular problems, psychiatric symptoms, AIDS, or other illnesses is necessarily repressing negative emotions. We have seen in the last two chapters that chronic overt hostility and expressed anger are dangerous harbingers of ill health.

Nevertheless, the relationship between emotional suppression and disease is clear enough to sensitize you to what some of your health problems may signal.

For example, the next time you find yourself with a "killer" headache, muscle spasms, or stomach pains, ask yourself if you are feeling angry or resentful but swallowing your negative emotions. If you notice that your immune system is rundown and you are falling prey to just about every virus, cold, or flu that's going around, ask yourself if there are negative feelings that you might be holding in and need to let go. If, like Joan, you get depressed, anxious, or overstressed, check out the possibility that you, too, are turning suppressed anger against yourself.

Your body's symptoms can function as an early warning system that can literally save your life. The appropriate expression of negative feelings requires both psychological awareness and good communication skills—both of which can be learned if the proper motivation exists.

In the final analysis, the most important requirements for dealing with negative feelings in a way that will be protective of your health are honesty and courage. These qualities lie within you, waiting only to be discovered, nurtured, and mobilized for action.

9

Thrills, Chills, and Ills

"I don't think I can take much more of this relationship," Jack told me. "I'm totally strung out at this point. I can't eat or sleep; I've lost ten pounds, and I can barely concentrate at the office, let alone do any worthwhile work. I know that I still love her, but unless she gets it together and decides that she definitely loves me and wants to get married, I'm getting out of this relationship once and for all."

In discussing his troubled relationship with Melanie, Jack was actually describing his addiction to her and to the chaos and drama of their on again/off again courtship.

Still a bachelor at 38, and after more than twenty years of dating hundreds of women, when Jack first met Melanie he believed that at last he had found the woman to marry. The attraction between them was immediate and powerful. The first three months of their relationship was, in Jack's words, "a perfect love story." That perfection quickly disappeared, however, when Melanie suddenly and inexplicably had a change of heart.

In his first therapy session, Jack described the turn of events this way: "Everything was going along beautifully—I was intoxicated with love and so was she. We were passionate, we told each other how incredible it was to have found each other, and we spoke very seriously of marriage. Then, in the course of just one week, with no prior warning, Melanie suddenly switched gears and started acting weird—withdrawn, sad, and cold.

"Before that time," Jack continued, "there were no significant or insurmountable problems as far as I was concerned. Look, I'm not naïve. I've been involved with enough women to know the signs of problems in a relationship when I see them, but this one totally blindsided me.

"Naturally, I was concerned by her low mood and insisted that she tell me what was wrong. But she refused to talk. So I assumed that it was a temporary depression due to something that had happened with a friend or relative or something at work. I decided to be patient until she was ready to discuss it.

"And then, one night, she just lowered the boom," Jack said. "She told me I was wrong for her; that she didn't really love me; that I'm a 'nice guy' and all, but that we're completely unsuited for each other and she wanted to start dating other guys. I was dumbfounded."

When Melanie broke off the relationship with Jack, he became agitated and depressed. His distress was so acute that he suffered sudden weight loss, insomnia, and severe headaches. Jack was referred to me by his doctor, who had become alarmed by the extent of his patient's anxiety and the change in his personality and behavior.

Jack's doctor observed, "Before their breakup, Jack was a remarkably cool, collected guy . . . a very sophisticated corporate type, highly intelligent, successful, smooth, and very much in control.

"But, since Melanie left him," the doctor continued, "Jack is a bundle of exposed nerve endings. The man's hands shake so much he can barely hold a glass of water. He can't sleep or eat.

If I didn't know Jack better, I'd swear he was withdrawing from cocaine or some other addiction."

The man I met on his first day of psychotherapy was no cool cucumber. Jack was, indeed, strung out, wildly anxious, and deeply depressed.

"I'm humiliated to behave like this," Jack admitted. "You don't know me, but I've never felt or looked like this in my life. I feel like I'm going to jump directly out of my skin. I don't think I can take it if I lose her." He moaned.

When I asked Jack to tell me about Melanie, he described her as the "ideal woman" for him: "She's elegant, sophisticated, funny, charming, sexy, and gorgeous." As he spoke of her, his eyes welled up with tears.

"During the three months that we were together, I felt great about myself. I knew that I had never fallen in love before. This is definitely the real thing for me. What I can't understand is what happened with her. How could she be so in love with me one day and so out of love the next?"

I asked Jack how he felt about himself without Melanie. "I feel worthless," he responded without hesitation. "I'm ashamed of how broken I am. I'm out of control and I can't stand the feeling. But the only thing that's going to stop this pain is for me to get her back. If I can't, I'm going to hate myself forever for losing the only woman who ever mattered to me."

Jack came for his second session a few days later and we spoke further of the intensity of his pain and need to win Melanie back. Then I didn't see Jack again until two months later.

I later learned that when Jack returned home from my office after that second session, there was a message on his answering machine from Melanie. They saw each other that night and Melanie proclaimed herself "a fool" for letting go of him. Since he got back what he most desired, Jack saw no further need for therapy.

As he later recounted the story, Melanie told him the night they reconciled, "I'm totally in love with you and I guess I just got scared. I couldn't bear the thought of going through an-other divorce [she had been married and divorced twice], and since you hadn't given me a ring yet, I assumed that you were unsure of your feelings about me. I'm so sorry. Please forgive me for hurting you."

When they got back together, Jack's withdrawal symptoms naturally were relieved. His depression not only abated, it was replaced by unbridled euphoria, at least initially. He told Mel-anie they would go shopping for an engagement ring very soon. However, although Jack's conscious misery disappeared, his anxiety failed to vanish.

"I wasn't shaking all the time and I regained my appetite," he told me. "But I just couldn't get myself to feel totally comfortable or secure with her. A little voice in my head kept warning me that what happened once could happen again. And, man, was I right!"

Six weeks after the first reconciliation, Melanie dropped bomb number two, this time despite the fact that Jack had formally proposed marriage. She recanted her proclamations of undying love. Once again she explained to Jack that he was unsuitable for her; that she was fond of him but not "in love"; that marriage with a man like him would be out of the question; and that it was time for them to go their separate ways.

This time, Jack implored Melanie to give him another chance. He told her that he would change in whatever ways she desired; that she was his ideal woman; that he would do anything in order to be deserving of her love; and that he simply could not live without her. In short, he begged.

Jack's attempts to keep the relationship together worked for only a few days, after which Melanie broke it off "for the last time." Added to her list of reasons now was the fact that he had begged to keep her, a behavior she interpreted as "weak and disgusting."

"I couldn't possibly love a man I can't respect," she told him. "You're too timid for me. I need a strong man who's in control of the relationship. You make me feel like I have to be in control, and that's not meeting my needs. It's over between us."

When Jack returned to therapy after the second breakup, he again was depressed, depleted, and out of control. "She's right, you know. I'm not the one in charge. I'd do anything not to lose her and, ironically, that's the very thing she's rejecting me for." However, Jack's self-blame was somewhat attenuated by his frustration and anger with Melanie.

"I still love her, there's no doubt about that," Jack admitted. "I'd go back to her in a heartbeat if I had the chance. But she's maddening. She doesn't make any sense to me. One day, I'm her one-and-only; the next day, I'm dog meat. How can a person's feelings change that much?

"Melanie says I'm the best person she's ever met," Jack continued with a bewildered expression, "and that I treat her better than any man she's ever known. Then, in the next breath, she tells me that I'm trying too hard to please her and I'm *too* nice! I just don't get it."

I asked Jack to explain why he would go back to her if given the opportunity, considering how confusing and painful the relationship was for him. He didn't hesitate to reply.

"Because when I'm with her and things are good between us, it's the greatest high I've ever known. I feel like my worth as a man is validated. The fact that a woman as fabulous as Melanie chooses to be with me is a statement about how attractive and valuable I must be. But when she rejects me, it's the worst low I've ever known."

Within a few months, Melanie recontacted Jack and they got together once again. The cycle repeated itself twice thereafter within the first year of their relationship.

Jack was an insightful and motivated patient who worked hard in therapy to understand himself better. He realized that, despite his current financial success, he had retained strong feelings of inadequacy as a result of being raised in a relatively poor, lower-class family. He understood that Melanie represented to him a level of social acceptability and status that he still deeply wished to reach. The carrot of marriage that she periodically dangled held the promise that he would finally feel "good enough" about himself.

Jack also understood that the relationship with Melanie was very exciting to him, albeit very painful. The ups and downs were so high and so low that he could evade the boredom and restlessness that he had experienced in other relationships. Jack was terrified of becoming like his parents, trapped in a deadening marriage that stifled not only their psychological growth but that of the entire family. Certainly, he told himself, marriage to Melanie could never be like his parents' life, since he would be continually challenged in order to "keep her interested."

Ultimately, though, Jack reached the point of recognition that the roller-coaster ride was becoming perilous to his health. He was issued regular warnings about the deterioration of his overall health by his doctor. And, with the exception of the first few weeks following each of his reconciliations with Melanie, most of the time Jack felt generally rundown.

Over the course of his turbulent relationship, Jack's self-confidence had waned considerably. His energy was so drained by the frustration of being continually rejected by a woman whom he seemed unable to stop loving and needing that there was virtually none left to direct toward his old hobbies, political involvements, and friendships. During the "off" periods with Melanie, Jack dated halfheartedly, but willingly dropped his new dates the moment she called to reactivate the addictive cycle.

Romantic Love and Uncertainty

Chronic anxiety, you will recall, is one of the Seven Deadly Signs that indicates a relationship is toxic. Why, then, would a man like Jack find such distressful feelings so irresistible? The answer lies in the connection between uncertainty and our cultural myth or notion of romantic love.

Romance, after all, is never portrayed in popular culture as a calm, stable, predictable affair. Indeed, if you give it some thought, you will realize that romantic love includes just about every emotion with one major exception: feelings of security and stability. In fact, the essence of romance is *uncertainty:* Will boy get girl? Will she marry the man she loves?

Romantic love involves exhilaration, exultation, intoxicating highs, passion, happiness, ecstasy, hope, and many other intensely positive experiences. The concept also includes negative feelings such as anger, sadness, deep pain, desperation, panic, high anxiety, self-doubt, rage, jealousy, revenge, and even hatred. So, the big highs and super lows are the stuff of romantic love. The world's greatest literary love stories—and probably your own experience—bear testimony to this fact.

But, in order for a love relationship to endure over time and for the partners to remain healthy both physically and psychologically, the instability of romantic love must resolve itself into another form that comprises stability, reliability, constancy, trust, security, and predictability. To distinguish this latter form of love from the romantic variety, let's call it *stable love.*

The presence of stable love does not mean that romance and excitement must necessarily disappear from marriage or other long-term relationships. On the contrary, while healthy, enduring marriages rest primarily on the underpinnings of stable love, successful partners remain able to ignite the positive aspects of the romantic mode when they so desire. Thus, stable love is an addition—an anchor—to romantic love, not a replacement for it.

Without that anchor, purely romantic love almost invariably turns toxic: The negative feelings begin to outweigh the positive, the involvement becomes draining and exhausting, the anxiety feels intolerable, and, in short, the whole thing stops being very much fun.

Jack interpreted the big highs and big lows of his experience with Melanie as evidence that he was finally "truly in love." Although he had read and heard about these kinds of feelings all his life, no one before Melanie had elicited this apex and abyss of strong emotion in Jack. He convinced himself that the acute anxiety and the continuous instability of the relationship were necessary to endure in order to reach the happy ending of his fantasies.

Moreover, since Jack feared stability as a precursor to the deadened state of his parents' type of marriage, he found himself stuck in the romantic mode, unable to insist that the bond with Melanie either transform into a more stable, predictable form or cease altogether.

Mislabeling Anxiety

Many of my patients have Lethal Lovers who perpetuate maddening uncertainty by continually creating chaos, drama, and crises in their relationships. My patients routinely rationalize their addictions by proclaiming, "At least the relationship isn't boring." In fact, they often describe their lovers or their relationships as exciting, challenging, stimulating, or fascinating. Only when pressed would these same people admit that their experiences are in fact riddled with anxiety and stress.

This illustrates that *how* you feel depends on the words you select to label your general physiological experience. Moreover, the labels you tend to use depend primarily on the *context* of that experience.

For example, imagine that you are sitting in a dentist's chair anticipating a lengthy and potentially painful procedure. Your physiological reactions most likely would include an increased heart rate, sweaty palms, dry mouth, nervous stomach, and somewhat shallow breathing. In the context of the sterile dentist's office, you would probably label your experience as anxiety or fear.

On the other hand, imagine that you are getting dressed to go out with a man or woman with whom you are falling in love, although neither of you has yet to declare your feelings. What physiological reactions would you now experience? Increased heart rate? Probably. Sweaty palms? Likely. Shallow breathing, nervous stomach, even dryness of the mouth? Yes, again. Only now the context of these reactions is completely different from that of the dentist's office. Consequently, you would be far more likely to label your feelings as *excitement* instead of *anxiety*. Nevertheless, despite the different contexts, the physiological cues of the two emotional states would be largely equivalent.

In love relationships of protracted instability and uncertainty, your tendency will be to label your feelings as excitement or arousal rather than anxiety or fear, due to the romantic context. Although Jack labeled his feelings negatively during breakup periods, he put a positive spin on his quite similar reactions during reconciliation periods. And, while he continued to suffer unhealthy levels of anxiety even when he was back together with Melanie, he described his anxiety and stress in more romantically acceptable terms such as "excitement," "stimulation," "challenge," and "fascination." Jack's mislabeling interfered with his ability to judge that the relationship was in fact harmful to his health until he was nearing a point of physical and emotional collapse.

The tendency to conform the emotional label to the context of experience accounts for why so many people, such as Jack, accept and tolerate toxic degrees of anxiety in addictive love relationships.

Addictive Love and the White Door

Remember, behavior is learned through the use of either positive or negative reinforcement. The latter involves the presentation of a painful or unpleasant stimulus that is then *removed* when the desired behavior is shown. The rat who was trained to run through the white door in order to turn off painful shocks was conditioned through negative reinforcement.

Positive reinforcement, on the other hand, involves the presentation of a pleasant, rewarding stimulus after the desired behavior has been displayed. The rat who learned to go through the white door in order to receive a wedge of cheese was conditioned through positive reinforcement.

Which model fits Jack's behavior and those of most other love addicts? On first glance, it might appear to be intermittent positive reinforcement. Jack, for example, would say that the reason he stays hooked on Melanie is because it feels so good to him to be with her when they are getting along well.

The truth, however, is that intermittent *negative* reinforcement drives Jack's addiction. Melanie's rejections produce panic states of painful, debilitating anxiety for Jack. The only thing that reduces his panic is getting back together with her.

During a breakup period, when Melanie calls Jack to suggest that they see each other "just to talk," Jack frantically "jumps through the white door" and presses for a reconciliation. Being accepted back by Melanie, then, alleviates his painfully high anxiety, thereby providing a powerful negative reinforcement for his behavior. In effect, Jack is *conditioned* to run back into Melanie's arms just as the rat runs through the white door to stop the painful shock.

Melanie retains control of Jack and of the relationship. As their dangerous dance unfolds, she faults him for being too weak and for running back to her whenever she crooks her finger. Ultimately, Jack will be rejected for his failure to be strong and to control the relationship. That rejection, of course, will explode Jack's anxiety into panic, which, once again, will be relieved when Melanie approaches him for yet another reconciliation. This is the dangerous, addictive dance of their toxic relationship.

Thus, romantic relationships that feed on uncertainty, unpredictability, and instability produce strong conditioned behaviors that often bewilder the very people who display them. Jack, for example, was at least as intrigued with his own "crazy behavior of going back" as he was with Melanie's actions. He, along with everyone who knew him, failed to understand what made him return to such a destructive relationship. What they failed to see is that Jack's behavior wasn't really the result of analytical thought or intentional decision. Instead, Jack's behavior was merely a conditioned response: He ran for the white door to turn off the pain of separation and withdrawal.

Hope Springs Eternal

While the capacity to invest hope and faith in other people is generally a health-promoting and protective trait, there are times when such feelings serve only to strengthen your addiction to a destructive, unstable relationship. Jack, for example, continued to hope that Melanie would change, despite all evidence to the contrary.

Over time, Melanie's continually disappointing behavior began to exact a considerable toll on Jack's self-esteem. This is because Jack defined the problems in the relationship—not always consciously or explicitly—as a measure of *his* abilities and self-worth. In other words, Jack believed that if *he* could only say and do the "right things," Melanie would develop a more stable personality.

Given his way of thinking, Melanie's failure to stabilize her feelings became, in Jack's mind, evidence of *his* inadequacies and shortcomings. After all, he erroneously reasoned, if he were stronger, smarter, more flexible, more attractive, etc., etc., then Melanie would be able to resolve her internal conflicts.

Thus, a secondary addictive pattern was established. Not only was Jack addicted through intermittent negative reinforcement patterns in the relationship, he also was hooked on the idea that *he* could somehow fix or cure Melanie, thereby awarding the romantic fantasy its happy ending. In this sense, Jack wasn't hooked on Melanie as much as he was on his own powers to make her finally, truly love him. Now, his ego had become invested in trying to make Melanie different.

When the Bad Outweighs the Good

Eventually, after sixteen months and a great deal of therapy, Jack determined to get off the roller coaster. Like many people who suffer from addictions of one kind or another, Jack was ready to disconnect from Melanie only when the bad things that were happening to him so outweighed whatever good he gained—when the pain overcame the pleasure—that no option remained other than to sever the tie if he was going to survive.

Unfortunately, though, that meant that Jack had "bottomed out," suffering from numerous deadly signs of relationship toxicity: depression, a profound sense of helplessness and loss of control, greatly lowered self-esteem, chronic anxiety, and, ultimately, raging anger both at himself and at Melanie. Of course, he suffered too from some of the physical symptoms that prolonged exposure to stress and toxic emotions can induce—chronic headaches, muscle spasms, and impaired sleep.

In order to sever the pernicious bond between them, Jack knew that he had to leave the relationship permanently, instead of succumbing to the conditioned relief of going back through the metaphorical white door. At my direction, Jack finally ceased all conversation and contact with Melanie, although the effort took enormous willpower. Jack had to work on relabeling his emotions—the love he felt was now called obsession and addiction; the excitement and challenge were more accurately labeled as anxiety and, ultimately, boredom.

It took Jack nearly another year after the final breakup to regain his former confidence and positive self-esteem. But the last time I saw him for a follow-up session, he was happily involved in a healthy, stable relationship for which a marriage date had been set.

"I had to get far, far away from Melanie to realize just how bad that relationship was for me," he reflected. "I feel like I almost died trying to please that woman. All I can say is thank heaven I got off that roller coaster in time before the car went completely off the track."

10

On the Horns of Ambivalence

Squinting at the digital alarm clock on her nightstand, Paul's wife read the time: 3:35 A.M. Then she recognized the sound that had disturbed her sleep. Paul was retching piteously in the bathroom. Dry heaves, she thought, since he hadn't been able to eat even a quarter of his dinner.

"That's it, Paul," she said as she entered the bathroom and turned on the light. "The minute the doctor's office opens this morning, I'm taking you there. You probably have an ulcer or something worse. You've got to get this thing checked out."

"Can't," Paul responded, wiping his mouth on a towel. "I've got another meeting with Jim at eight o'clock this morning." Beads of perspiration covered his ashen face. "Man, I feel sick," he added.

"Look," his wife, Annette, replied, "as far as I'm concerned, it's Jim who's making you so sick. That and all this financial pressure."

"You're probably right," Paul answered. "I'm sorry I woke

you again. I'll try to see the doctor in the afternoon. Maybe he can give me something for my nerves."

"Okay. But promise me you'll go?"

"Yeah, I'll go. You go back to sleep. I'll be there in a few minutes."

Paul walked out to the living room and sat on the sofa, head in hands. Then he started pacing, wondering for the hundredth time, it seemed, how to get out of the mess he had created. As soon as daylight broke and he checked to assure himself that Annette and his two children were still asleep, he called his lover, Celeste.

"I'm sorry I woke you, sweetheart," Paul said in response to her sleepy hello. "What's the name of that psychologist? I need to talk to someone."

Later that afternoon, Paul came to see me.

"I'm losing my grip," he began. "My wife thinks the problem is with my business partner and best friend, Jim; Jim thinks the problem is in my marriage—he knows about Celeste; and Celeste thinks the problem is with her."

"What do *you* think?" I asked.

"I know what the problem is." Paul pointed at his heart and said, "It's with me. I'm so screwed up, my heart is breaking and my mind is close behind. In a sense, I love all three of them—Jim, Celeste, and my wife. But at the same time I resent the hell out of all of them. I have to make some decisions and do something to straighten out my life. I can't sit on this fence anymore."

I appreciated Paul's candor and clearly saw the extent of his pain. As his story unfolded, I began to understand that he was indeed impaled on the horns of ambivalence.

Jim and Paul had been best friends for nearly twelve years. Eight years earlier, they had formed a partnership and bought a restaurant-supply business. Because of their friendship, they naïvely and unwisely omitted from their contract a specification of terms for dissolving the partnership, despite their attorney's strong admonitions to the contrary.

Although the business did reasonably well for five years, the last three had been very difficult. Paul believed that he and Jim were "buddies" and, in his words, "that we would either make it together or go belly-up together." But Jim saw things differently. Pressed for cash and apparently unwilling to share a failure with his friend, Jim had gone to an outside source to raise the necessary capital to buy Paul out of the business.

"I can't believe the guy is doing this to me," Paul said. "He was my best man, and I was his; he's the godfather to my kids; his wife and mine are best friends, too. I don't want to lose him—he's like family to me—but this is a total betrayal. He's screwing me out of my own business. He knows I can't raise the money to buy him out, and the price he's giving me isn't half of what the business was worth before the recession."

Suddenly Paul jumped out of the chair in my office and excused himself to go to the bathroom. He returned a few minutes later, pale and shaken.

"I'm sorry," he apologized, "but this is what's happening to me. My stomach and my nerves are shot to hell."

Before we continued, Paul agreed to consult with his physician the next day. Then, assuring me that he felt well enough, he proceeded.

"So I don't know whether to love or hate Jim. I feel both. But that's only one part of my story. What's really killing me is that *I'm* a liar and a cheat. I've been married for ten years to Annette. She loves me; she's a good woman and a devoted mother. But there's no passion left in our marriage. I don't think we have anything to really talk about. I'm lonely when I'm with her.

"I met Celeste at a chamber of commerce cocktail party six months ago," Paul continued. "Don't get the wrong idea about her. She didn't even know I was married. Initially, I lied to her, too. The first two weeks I knew her, Annette and the kids were out of town, so I was able to date her as though I were a single guy. I don't wear a wedding band, and I guess I pulled off the charade, since she never even asked if I was married.

"If you want to know the truth, I make myself sick with how good a liar I am," Paul admitted. "But once we had made love and I felt sure she was pretty involved emotionally, I told her about Annette and the kids. She was very pissed off at first, wouldn't take my calls or see me for about ten days. Then, when she agreed to have lunch with me, I made up another story about how I was planning to leave Annette in the near future. I begged her to hang in there with me until I could go through with a divorce. I told her my business problems had to be settled before I could leave my marriage.

"Now, three months later, I'm still married, Celeste's in love with me, and she's getting pretty strung out too. I can't face myself in the mirror. I want to come clean with Annette and tell her about Celeste, but I know it'll kill her. She'll kick me out, and I don't think I'm ready to leave my kids and marriage.

"And, just to show you what a terrific guy I really am, this isn't the first time I've been unfaithful," Paul said sarcastically. "I've been fooling around for years. But I've never fallen in love before, or even come close. So, in my mind, those were relatively meaningless episodes that never threatened my marriage. But I think I really do love Celeste. I've got to make some decisions or I'm going to fall apart. The guilt is killing me. I can't stand the pressure of making up stories to Annette, sneaking around, and lying to Celeste half the time, too.

"My life's a total mess," he concluded. "I need you to help me figure out what I want. I can't live this way anymore."

A few days later I consulted with Paul's physician, who confirmed that Paul was "somaticizing"—translating his severe psychological conflicts into physical symptoms. His stomach problems were somewhat eased with medication, and the doctor said he detected no signs of an ulcer.

Nevertheless, Paul had to cancel his next three scheduled appointments with me when his lower back went into acute spasm. X-rays revealed a possible disk problem, and the orthopedist confined Paul to total bed rest with muscle relaxants and painkillers around the clock.

"Well," Paul laughed halfheartedly when he spoke to me by telephone, "at least I won't get myself into any more trouble with women. I can't even move."

Ambivalence, Conflict, and Anxiety

Paul's life crisis and physical symptoms graphically illustrate the effects of inner emotional turmoil on the body. In a very real sense, his ambivalence—the psychological conflicts—about the most important relationships in his life had, at least temporarily, nearly paralyzed him.

The notion that unresolved inner conflict forms the wellspring for anxiety permeates almost every major psychological theory from psychoanalysis to contemporary behaviorism. One model, particularly applicable to Paul's situation, characterizes anxiety as the result of three fundamental forms of conflict: First, *approach-approach conflicts* occur when you feel caught between two opposing goals, both of which you desire; second, *avoidance-avoidance conflicts* occur when you feel caught between two outcomes, both of which you seek to elude; and third, *approach-avoidance conflicts* occur when you simultaneously desire and spurn the same goal.

Paul is the victim of all three forms of primary conflict. He feels the simultaneous desire to stay with his wife and family *and* to be with his lover. Since Celeste will no longer tolerate being the "other woman," Paul must choose between two opposing but desirable goals, thereby placing him in an approach-approach conflict.

Another way to view Paul's romantic dilemma is as an avoidance-avoidance conflict. In this sense, Paul does not want to lose his marriage and family, nor does he want to lose his lover. Since successfully avoiding the loss of either relationship necessarily will result in losing the other, he again feels overwhelmed by anxiety.

Paul's relationship with Jim is yet another source of conflict and anxiety. This case is an example of an approach-avoidance conflict. On one hand, he strongly desires to maintain his long and close friendship with Jim—the approach side of the conflict. On the other hand, he feels a strong push to accuse Jim of treachery and betrayal and to terminate their friendship along with the partnership—the avoidance portion.

107

Paul's intense anxiety, then, is the cumulative effect of the three psychological conflicts in which he is embroiled. The degree of his discomfort is a function of both the number of conflicts he faces and the importance of each in his life.

Paul is caught on the horns of ambivalence—a paralyzing state of vacillation, indecision, and uncertainty. The strength of his ambivalence results from the fact that the psychological "pull" of the opposing goals in his various conflicts are about equally strong.

The Psychosomatic Connection

Paul's case is a classic, textbook study of psychosomatic illness. This does not mean that his stomach and back spasms are mental inventions or fictions. On the contrary, Paul's physical problems are very real and very painful. It does mean, however, that Paul's psychological turmoil has translated itself into physical symptoms. In an intriguing way, Paul's body is forcing him to resolve his ambivalence.

Just as Paul's psyche feels pulled in multiple and conflicting directions by his complex issues, simultaneously many of the large muscle groups in his body are being yanked in opposing directions. This physical tension produces the spasms. Paul's symptoms illustrate the fact that the body cannot or does not differentiate between psychological images (thoughts) and physical realities (events).

It is actually quite an impressive feat that the body can respond to mental phenomena. Numerous studies have demonstrated that pure visual imagery stimulates physiological processes identical to those that would be activated by actual events. For example, by attaching electrodes to muscles, scientists can show that athletes who merely visualize themselves running or jumping actually contract the appropriate muscles in response to their mental images.

So, as Paul engages in a mental struggle over his various life conflicts, his body—specifically, the muscles in his lower back and stomach—perform a simultaneous, parallel struggle. It is this intricate link between the mind's work and the body's response that is meant by the psychosomatic connection.

Ambivalence and Mixed Messages

To be sure, Paul is not the unwitting victim of other people's actions. Clearly, he has played a major role in creating many of the interpersonal problems that plague him. Moreover, viewed from the vantage point of either Annette or Celeste, Paul readily might be tagged a Lethal Lover.

However, from Paul's perspective, his ambivalence is, to some degree, a reaction to the ways in which the other people—his wife, his lover, and his best friend—have treated *him*. In the case of each relationship, Paul is able to describe ways in which he has been given conflicting communications, both verbal and nonverbal, that contribute to his inner conflicts.

For example, Paul describes Annette as a loving and devoted wife. But Paul also complains that over the eight years of their marriage, Annette had physically "let herself go completely." She had gained more than sixty pounds and, since she stayed home most days with the kids, she wore only baggy sweat suits, no makeup, and she rarely bothered to do her hair. Annette had become less attractive not only in Paul's eyes but in her own perception. Because she was overweight and felt unattractive, Annette made no effort to initiate sex with her husband, nor was she receptive to his overtures.

On the other hand, Annette was loyal and caring; she took excellent care of their children and maintained a lovely home. But to Paul, the nature of Annette's love had transformed from that of a wife toward her husband to that of an Earth Mother to the entire family, including him. The motherly love she displayed toward Paul was anathema to his sexual feelings toward her.

Acknowledging her laxness in attending to her physical attractiveness and sense of sexuality, Annette told Paul on a number of occasions that she expected him to understand that she was going through a phase and therefore to tolerate the lack of sexual love between them until she was ready to change and "get it together" at some indeterminate time in the future. She assured him that she wanted to change, although she took no action to do so. Moreover, she indicated in no uncertain terms that any infidelity on Paul's part would not be tolerated. In fact, on more than a few occasions, Annette insisted on departing early from parties they were attending because of what she detected as flirting between Paul and other women.

Paul interprets Annette's behavior and expectations as a set of mixed messages that create the basis for his ambivalence.

"She expects me to be utterly devoted and faithful to her," he explained, "as she seems to be to me. I'm supposed to just put my sexual needs on a shelf somewhere. But I keep myself very fit and I pride myself on maintaining the best physical appearance I can. And, at the risk of immodesty, I know that I'm an attractive guy.

"On one hand," Paul continued, "Annette puts her foot down about other women—and I don't blame her—but on the other hand, she seems to be testing me. She seems to be *trying* to look awful and to turn me and herself completely off sexually. She's not doing anything to improve her appearance or our sexual situation. At the same time, she's watching me like a hawk to be sure that I don't even look at other women. I feel like the whole thing is a big setup. She makes me feel torn between staying faithful to her and being with my lover."

Paul also perceives a striking contradiction between Celeste's actions and words. The incongruity is frustrating and confusing to him and therefore adds to the intensity of his inner conflicts.

"Here's what Celeste does," Paul explained. "First, she takes a real tough stand about not wanting to be involved with a married man. And, to tell you the truth, I not only respect her position, I wish she would stick with it. Instead, she tells me that she won't be the 'other woman' or participate in adultery, but as she's saying these noble words, she's kissing me, unzipping my pants, and obviously seducing me.

"Now, I realize that I can choose to listen to her words and resist her actions," he admitted. "But I'm only human, and, frankly, the lack of sex at home makes me entirely too vulnerable. Celeste so totally turns me on when she starts with the seduction, I'm a complete 'goner.'

"What really gets me upset is that when the lovemaking is over and I'm just relaxing, she starts laying all the demands on me again. 'You have to tell your wife,' she says; 'I can't put up with being the hidden woman you can only see during your breaks from the office'; or, 'If you don't leave Annette, I'm leaving you!' "

Again, from Paul's perspective, his inner conflict is being fueled by what he perceives as Celeste's ambivalence.

"I've got to be honest," Paul explained. "If Celeste stuck to her guns and refused to continue our relationship, my choices would seem much clearer. But even though she pays lip service to not wanting to have an affair with a married man, she continues to do it. So, I can keep putting off making a decision. Sometimes I think that Celeste secretly likes the fact that I'm not really hers. Many times I've wondered if she'd still be there for me if I did leave Annette."

Finally, Paul perceives Jim as having what he calls "two contradictory personalities." One is that of his long-standing best friend; the guy he can trust above anyone else; the friend to whom he has confided his innermost thoughts, including the details of his affair with Celeste and his confused feelings toward Annette. The other side of Jim is the ruthless business-man who'd just as soon sell his partner down the river as he would a complete stranger or his worst enemy.

"I don't know how to reconcile these two personalities," Paul explained. "If he would totally turn against me as a friend, I wouldn't feel the tug inside to maintain the relationship. Even after screwing me in business, Jim tells me that, as *his* best friend, he expects me to understand and support *him!* You know, when I'm away from him and talking with Annette about the business, I can get really angry at Jim. But as soon as I come face to face with the guy over some issue where I need to take a hard stance that might damage his financial position but protect my own, I can't do what I know I should. The part of me that wants to hold on to my best friend absolutely paralyzes me."

Paul's *perception* of ambivalent feelings in his wife, lover, and partner perpetuates his painful indecision and inner turmoil. Naturally, each of the players in his story would likely say the same of Paul: that *his* ambivalence is what evokes the mixed messages they seem to give him. In this sense, then, ambivalent feelings produced by unresolved inner conflict are not only toxic but often contagious.

Dependency and Ambivalence

Romantic love relationships are not the exclusive arena for ambivalence or for the dangerous, harmful behavior that conflicted feelings can produce. In fact, one of the most fertile grounds for breeding toxic ambivalence is parent-child relationships.

Toby and Roberta, for example, are mother and daughter and business partners as well. Toby divorced her husband when Roberta, an only child, was just 5 years old. The father, an extremely handsome but immature and irresponsible man, abandoned Toby and their child and moved to New York, leaving them to fend for themselves in Los Angeles. Although Toby is an especially attractive woman, she never remarried. Indeed, she refused even to date until Roberta was 18 and living at college.

Toby sacrificed her personal happiness in the name of her daughter. In part, that devotion derived from the profound sense of guilt she harbored for the fact that Roberta was raised without a father. She never forgave herself for being "stupid enough to marry such a loser." As an atonement for her mistaken judgment, Toby vowed to raise Roberta alone, and to be both mother and father to her child so that no man could ever again leave her and her daughter heartbroken and abandoned.

By the age of 18, Roberta's feelings toward her mother had

become quite complex. Roberta clearly loved and admired Toby for trying so hard to compensate for the absence of a father in her life. But she felt smothered by the closeness of their relationship and longed to establish her independence and separateness from her consuming mother. Moreover, Roberta resented her mother for instilling in her a fundamental distrust of all men and for making her feel guilty about the fact that Toby had never remarried.

On her part, Toby was quick to remind Roberta of all the sacrifices she had made for her. She regularly admonished her daughter "not to make the same mistake I did, by becoming dependent on any man."

However, Roberta dropped out of college after one year when she fell in love with a handsome ski instructor. She moved to the ski resort where he lived and, within six months, became pregnant. The boyfriend panicked at the thought of marriage and fatherhood and implored Roberta to get an abortion. But Roberta wanted her baby and decided to give up the man.

So, Roberta moved home to her mother, gave birth to a baby girl, and proceeded to replicate her mother's lonely life. But she needed a way to support herself and her daughter financially. Given her limited education and work experience, plus the competing demands of motherhood, Roberta's job options were few.

Then, Toby made her an offer she couldn't refuse. As the owner of a successful temporary employment agency, Toby proposed giving Roberta a partnership interest in the business and a position as general manager.

The relationship between mother and daughter, complex from the beginning, now developed several additional layers of mutual dependency, complication, and ambivalence. Roberta loved her mother, as always, but now she needed her in more ways than she could even enumerate, much less tolerate. Toby provided Roberta and her granddaughter with a place to live and went home before Roberta from the office nearly every evening to cook the family dinner. "It was really no trouble,"

Toby claimed, since she was "accustomed to making sacrifices."

While Roberta was dependent on her mother in their business relationship, Toby was dependent on Roberta as well, since, for the first time in twenty years of her business, Toby felt she had a trusted partner on whom she could rely. Moreover, since Toby suffered from recurrent bouts of painful rheumatoid arthritis, she frequently took days off due to flare-ups of her condition, during which Roberta's workload doubled.

Like her mother had done as a single parent, Roberta shunned relationships with men. She too didn't want to get hurt by another "selfish, lousy guy," so she relied entirely on Toby to provide the only sense of family and security her own little girl had ever known.

Toby was delighted to be so needed again by Roberta and, now, by her precious granddaughter. She was pleased that her business would remain in the family if and when she ever carried through on her threats to retire.

At the same time, though, Toby bitterly complained about her loss of freedom and privacy, saying things like, "Just as I was getting used to having some time of my own and some peace and quiet, I have a baby all over again." Despite her satisfaction at being able to offer Roberta both a career and a stake in the business, Toby was continually critical of her daughter's management style and business judgments as well as her child-rearing philosophy and practice. Since Toby retained the controlling interest in the business, Roberta was answerable to her mother for all her decisions and actions. This arrangement soon became a point of serious contention between them.

Notwithstanding the fact that Toby demanded long working hours of her daughter, she constantly warned Roberta of the "dangers of being all work and all mother, since you'll wind up just like me—old, bitter, and lonely." Then Toby would add, "Besides, you need to find yourself a wealthy man who can take care of you and your old mother so I'll be off the hook." She said this repeatedly, despite her lifelong admonishment not to become dependent on a man.

Roberta and Toby came for joint therapy, simultaneously enraged with each other and remaining affectionate and protective of each other.

"There is no doubt in my mind that my mother utterly loves me," Roberta explained during a private session. "And I do appreciate everything she's done for me. But Mom loves me with strings attached. I always feel obligated to repay her or make it all up to her. All my life I've felt responsible for the fact that Mom never remarried. Now, I'm a grown woman and mother, and I'm more dependent on her than ever. I'm grateful for her help—but I resent her a lot for making me need her so much.

"The worst part," Roberta continued, "is that Mom makes me feel guilty for causing her the stress that brings on her arthritis. So I can't ever get angry or say what's on my mind because if she gets upset about what I have to say, I'll be responsible for causing her pain."

Roberta and Toby have a highly ambivalent mother-daughter bond that is both intensely positive and strongly negative. Naturally, the incongruity of those competing emotions creates significant internal conflict for both of them. That inner turmoil, in turn, contributes to exacerbations of Toby's arthritic condition as well as to Roberta's numerous anxiety-related skin problems, temporal mandibular joint syndrome (TMJ)—pain in her face and jaw—and irritable bowel syndrome.

The source of their ambivalence is the complex, multilevel dependency between them. In a sense, Roberta needs her mother too much and in ways that are inappropriate for a grown woman with a child of her own. For example, Roberta still lives at home at the age of 32. She seeks her mother's approval for every clothing purchase she makes and for almost all her other decisions as well. When that approval is withheld by Toby, as it often is, Roberta becomes sullen and depressed.

Roberta's dependency is compounded by a business arrangement in which her mother has become the sole source of her present and future financial security. And, to the extent that Roberta attempts to have any social life whatsoever, she depends on her mother to babysit.

However, Roberta's dependency isn't one-sided. On her end, Toby relies on Roberta for fulfillment of numerous needs, many of which also are inappropriate. For example, Roberta and her granddaughter give Toby a sense that she is needed and a rationalization that she still has no time or energy for a man. "Besides," she says, "Roberta and the baby are all the family I'll ever need."

So, Toby needs Roberta in order to feel needed herself. Toby also needs Roberta to correct the mistakes that she made in her own life. In other words, her continual push for Roberta to marry a wealthy man appears to be more Toby's fantasy than her daughter's. At the same time, though, Toby supplies a potent dose of conflicting messages. For example, she reminds Roberta that the reason she built the business was so that her daughter could inherit it and never have to rely on a man for money. Further, on the rare occasions when Roberta has a date with an eligible man, Toby finds numerous faults with the fellow on the basis of only a brief meeting.

In therapy, Toby and Roberta worked on redefining their relationship so that much of the positive interdependence could remain, while a sorely needed degree of psychological separation also could be achieved. Roberta moved from her mother's house into her own apartment. She learned to be more selective about the things that she confided to her mother and to stop seeking Toby's approval for every move she made.

A formal business contract was written that spelled out Roberta's management role and increasing financial interest in the company over the course of seven years. In addition, they agreed to limit business discussions to the office so that their personal relationship as mother and daughter would be less contaminated.

In many respects, Toby and Roberta enjoyed a relationship that benefited them both in healthy, positive ways. They were close as a family unit and were each other's best friends as well. Their business arrangement, on balance, was advantageous to them both.

The task for Toby and Roberta, with the aid of therapy, was to ferret out and eliminate those elements of their relationship that were not healthy—the inappropriate dependency that bred resentment; the manipulative communication ("If you didn't aggravate me so much I wouldn't be sick"); and the mixed messages that aroused ambivalence ("Go out with men but stay home with me").

As Toby and Roberta successfully worked through the issues that caused them the greatest ambivalence, both reported feeling much less anxious, and their physical symptoms greatly decreased. As the negativity diminished along with the destructive ambivalence, the pleasure that both could derive from their special bond was far greater and beneficial to their health and to the well-being of the child they were raising.

One of the most insightful breakthroughs in Roberta's therapy came when she realized that she had reacted to her former boyfriend, who was the father of her child, very much as she did to her mother. Roberta recognized that in both cases, she was the object of the other person's ambivalence.

While Toby enjoyed being needed, she also complained about her loss of independence and privacy. While she encouraged Roberta to live with her in order to save money, Toby also continually suggested that Roberta get a life of her own. And, while Toby sometimes praised Roberta at the office, she also was quick to criticize and correct her mistakes, frequently in the presence of employees, which caused Roberta both embarrassment and consternation.

Toby's ambivalence made Roberta feel simultaneously accepted and rejected; needed and resented; appreciated and devalued.

Roberta described a parallel set of contradictory feelings in response to her former boyfriend. "Maybe that was the reason I fell in love with him . . . because he reminded me of my mother," she mused in a therapy session.

117

Roberta's therapeutic turning point came when she realized the intensely negative effects on her self-esteem that resulted from being the object of another person's ambivalence. She understood that by allowing herself to perpetuate any relationship in which the other person felt and behaved ambivalently toward her, she was devaluing herself and consequently courting a significant and inevitable depression.

Indeed, there is no more vulnerable and potentially dangerous position than to be the object of another person's ambivalence, especially in a love relationship. The psychological message of that emotional uncertainty is that there must be something wrong or flawed with *you,* otherwise your partner's feelings wouldn't be so conflicted. While intellectually you may be able to see that your partner's ambivalence is more about him or her than about you, the devastation to *your* self-esteem is nevertheless inescapable.

Ambivalence and Ill Health

As a general rule, relationships are neither entirely positive nor completely negative. By virtue of being human, people have flaws and shortcomings that, to varying degrees, create flaws and shortcomings in relationships. Thus, some ambivalence seems an inevitable emotional component of virtually every human bond.

If ambivalence is a part of most relationships, when and how does it become toxic? The defining criteria are how intense and how chronic the ambivalence is. At relatively low levels and on only a periodic or intermittent basis, ambivalence is unlikely to be very harmful.

However, when the intensity is high and the ambivalence is chronic, damage to the relationship and to the health and self-esteem of the individuals involved can be great. Ambivalence becomes intense when the positive emotional aspects are nearly equal to the negative. When the two competing poles are closely matched, the internal conflict is strong and the inner turmoil severe.

If, for example, the good things about your relationship are terrific and tremendously important in your system of values, while the bad things are comparatively minor, your ambivalence will be low. Consequently, you are unlikely to experience the discomfort of internal conflict over the relationship. Similarly, if the bad things in a relationship are terrible and greatly outweigh whatever is good about it, little conflict should exist and, in fact, the relationship would quite likely terminate.

On the other hand, if the good things are very good and numerous, and the bad things are very bad and numerous, you could well find yourself on the horns of ambivalence—a dilemma fraught, as you have seen, with emotional turmoil, anxiety, depression, and the myriad psychological symptoms and physical illnesses that toxic emotions produce.

The other prevailing variable in determining whether your ambivalence about a relationship—or your partner's ambivalence about you—is likely to damage your health is its frequency. Once in a while, almost everyone has a few misgivings or ambivalent feelings about even their most significant relationships. Periodically, a major problem may erupt that creates greater uncertainty. But as long as the ambivalent feelings are resolved and remain relatively infrequent, their damage is likely to be minimal.

However, if chronic ambivalence becomes the predominant emotional theme of your relationship, persistent stress and anxiety are the predictable results, with all their attendant damage to your physical and psychological health.

So, if you can say that you and your partner feel pretty sure about each other most of the time, toxic ambivalence is not likely to be present. But if you or your partner feels unsure about the relationship a lot of the time, then: Beware.

11

Learned Helplessness

I remember the first day I met Patricia. She was quite visibly nervous, with trembling hands and a quivering mouth. Nevertheless, she projected a sweet smile. But just beneath that surface smile was a depth of sadness and emotional vulnerability that remains etched in my memory for its poignancy.

Stan, Patricia's husband, accompanied her for that first session. He wasted no time in announcing that he was there "to help explain Patricia's problems." He predicted that "she probably would become too emotional and upset to think straight or to remember things accurately" so he'd thought it best to come along the first time.

Stan also made it perfectly clear that he had "nothing to do with Patricia's problems." He was, in his own perception, "a loving and understanding husband" who felt very bad that Patricia was going through so much difficulty and pain.

However, Stan further made clear that "Patricia's inability to function adequately in her duties as wife and mother because of her emotional instability" had become a source of consider-able inconvenience and irritation to him.

Finally, Stan admonished that "your [my] job," as Patricia's new therapist, was "to cure her" so that his inconvenience would be abated. During all of Stan's introductory remarks, Patricia sat on the opposite end of the couch, wringing her hands and crying silently, though still smiling sweetly, but never responding verbally.

When I asked Patricia to explain *her* reasons for seeking psychotherapy, she replied, "Stan's right. I've let him down as a wife and mother. I'm too nervous and emotional. I keep trying to change. I want to make him happy, but I guess it's no use. He deserves a better woman than me."

Initially, Patricia's pathetic response stood unchallenged by Stan. He merely nodded. Then, almost as an afterthought, he reached out to pat her hand and said, "No, Patty, I don't want another woman. I just want you to figure out why you make yourself so unhappy. You know what a good life we have— we're very well off financially, and we have two nice kids and a beautiful home. I've hired you a full-time, live-in housekeeper to help you out and it still doesn't make you happy. I don't know what else a man can do." A note of anger had crept into Stan's otherwise carefully controlled tone.

Again, Patricia agreed with Stan, confirming "how good Stan is to me" and "what a selfish, ungrateful person I must seem to him."

The session continued for another half-hour or so, although the dynamic of Patricia and Stan's marriage had been clearly illuminated within the first five minutes. At the session's close, Stan indicated that he would be available to speak with me anytime in the future "if it would help Patricia" but that he personally, emphatically, "had no need for therapy."

Once again, Patricia concurred. Only this time, in her agree-ment, I detected a ray of hope for our work together. "I think it would be much better if I could come in alone and talk with you from now on," she said. "But, of course, if Stan thinks he needs to talk to you about me, that's fine. He always explains things much better than I do," she added.

Patricia's tone implied that if she and I could just be alone, she might be able to tell me more honestly how she felt about the circumstances of her life. Moreover, since she obviously was deeply depressed and very receptive to therapy, I was certainly willing to work with her individually.

During the first six weeks of Patricia's therapy, the picture of her twelve-year marriage to Stan was fleshed out, this time from her perspective. Not surprisingly, her story was consistent with the impression the couple had created in that remarkable first five minutes of their initial session together.

In those early weeks, Patricia also told me a good deal about her parents, her life before she'd met Stan, and the development and course of her depressive illness during the two years prior to her coming to see me. Patricia recalled her parents' marriage as "a good one," describing her mother as an extremely dependent woman who defined her purpose in life as making her husband and children happy. This objective, Patricia explained, was not always easy since her father was a moody, controlling man who often berated his wife and two daughters for being "silly girls."

"I think I grew up as a pretty happy kid," Patricia recalled, "although I was always afraid of upsetting my dad. When I think about it, I can see that I'm basically a carbon copy of my mother. And Stan is a lot like my father. He's critical and controlling in the same way and he makes me feel stupid the way my dad did.

"The hardest thing to deal with," Patricia continued, "is that all I ever wanted to be was a real good mother and wife like Mom. But, despite everything I've tried—and I've tried *everything*—Stan *never* makes me feel like I'm doing a good enough job.

"He comes home nearly every night very stressed and moody from his day. He gets nasty with me as soon as he comes through the front door. That makes me very upset and I usually start crying and retreat to our bedroom. Then Stan becomes annoyed with me for being overly emotional. He says I'm setting a terrible example for the kids.

"I'm sure he's right, but I just can't help myself. Nothing I try to do ever makes him happy. I'm the world's biggest perfectionist myself, so it doesn't help when Stan points out my shortcomings. I know how inadequate I am without his reminding me all the time."

Patricia so feared her husband's moodiness and temper that she tragically said she would prefer "being physically abused rather than take any more of Stan's verbal abuse." The stories Patricia recounted about her life with Stan painted him as cold, unaffectionate, sexually withdrawn, inattentive, and uncommunicative.

Remarkably, though, Patricia's explanations for the troubles in her marriage centered entirely on *her* flaws and shortcomings. Her self-punitive style had produced a deadening depression punctuated only by feelings of helplessness and hopelessness.

"It's all my fault, I know," Patricia said. "There's a lot wrong with me. I *am* too emotional; I suppose I'll always be that way. I'm sure my feelings *do* get hurt too easily. Stan tries his hardest and I've just let him down. No man would be happy with me. I never do anything right. Nothing I try ever works to make things better between us. I want to be a perfect wife and mother, I really do, but I'm a total failure."

Despite her unhappiness, Patricia categorically rejected any notion of separating from Stan. At the same time, she was adamant that Stan would not participate in marital therapy and that he would never change. Thus, Patricia saw no options outside of her present, unhappy situation.

"He says the problems are mine, and I know he's right," she continued. "I guess I've really given up. Sometimes, I think the only way out of the pain is to take my own life, but I wouldn't do that to the kids. I guess I have to learn how to accept my situation without getting so upset and just stop expecting anything more from Stan."

Learned Helplessness and Depression

Patricia's passive acceptance of highly negative circumstances reveals a potentially lethal psychological state known as *learned helplessness*. Patricia had learned to believe that her problems were unsolvable because she viewed her actions as futile. As a consequence, she became too passive, fearful, and depleted to consider alternative actions or other interpretations of her life situation.

Learned helplessness occurs as a result of an aversive experience, or series of experiences over time, that leads you to *believe* that nothing you can do will relieve your pain and problems; and that your actions, no matter what they are, will simply not work to bring you what you want. Moreover, the experiences teach you to expect that, in future situations, your actions once again will be futile.[12]

Learned helplessness is the bleak psychological mindset that lies at the core of defeat and failure as well as a powerful paradigm for clinical depression. It explains how repeated experiences with failure and defeat can beat people down into a state of futility, hopelessness, helplessness, self-loathing, and even suicidal thoughts and/or actions like the one Patricia had so sadly assumed.

Learned helplessness was first demonstrated in a now-classic study in which dogs were given a mild electrical shock that they were helpless to escape. Later, when conditions were altered to allow the dogs to escape, the researchers were amazed to witness the dogs lying down, whimpering, and refusing to move. They simply gave up.[13]

The researchers deduced—and later conclusively proved with other subjects, including humans—that the dogs had been taught that their actions were futile. They had learned to be helpless as a generalized behavior.

What do experimental dogs and people like Patricia have in common? A great deal, as you have probably already realized. Patricia is emotionally yoked to Stan via her dependence on him. When Stan takes out his negative moods on Patricia, she is subjected to a negative experience over which she has no direct control and from which she believes she cannot escape. After years of trying futilely to change Stan, Patricia believes that she is helpless to affect his moods or behavior. Moreover, since Stan's habit is to punish his wife with temper outbursts and verbal abuse when he has had a bad day, his stress creates Patricia's emotional pain.

Pessimism, Explanatory Style, and Depression

Researchers have found that not all subjects evidence the familiar pattern of learned helplessness when they find out that their responses don't matter. Nor does every subject develop signs of depression in response to defeat and failure. In fact, some people deal with defeat only as a transitory setback. Consequently, they are able to bounce back with considerable emotional resilience after a failure instead of succumbing to a protracted, debilitating depression.

What distinguishes people who respond to negative experiences by feeling helpless from those who effectively resist depression? The answer lies in how the reasons for negative events are explained or interpreted. This critical, variable "explanatory style" states that a *pessimistic* explanatory style produces hopelessness, helplessness, and crippled self-esteem; whereas an *optimistic* explanatory style breeds faith in the future, adaptive coping, and healthy self-esteem.[14]

Pessimistic people often are knocked down for the count by life's adversities, becoming depressed because they explain the negative events that befall them in three specific ways: First, they attribute the cause of the bad event to something that is *permanent*—something that will always be that way. Second, they attribute negative events to causes that are *pervasive*.

When permanent and pervasive causes are given for the negative events that occur in life, hopelessness follows. After all, if the reasons are permanent and expected to exist across a variety of situations, how can you have hope that anything will be different in the future?

Third, the pessimist sees the cause of the bad event as lying *within himself* rather than with factors outside of him. This "internalized" explanation for a negative event injures and potentially debilitates self-esteem.

In contrast, the optimistic explanatory style attributes bad events to reasons that are *temporary, specific to the situation,* and *external.*

As a classic pessimist, Patricia *feels* hopeless because she explains her unhappy marriage as being due to causes that are *permanent, pervasive,* and *internal.* She describes herself as "a failure," claims that she is "too emotional," and alleges that she will "always be that way." These attributions imply permanence. There is no allowance in her thinking for the possibility that her responses might be transitory and temporary, arising out of the particular situation in which she finds herself with Stan.

Patricia proceeds to discount the notion that another man might respond to her differently. "No man," she says, "would be happy with me." She further asserts that "I never do anything right." So, Patricia's explanations for her unhappiness with Stan are pervasive as well as permanent.

The permanence and pervasiveness related in Patricia's explanations for her marital problems, then, leave her feeling helpless and hopeless—the essential conditions of depression. And, she completes the pessimistic triad by placing the reasons for her marital failure squarely on her own shoulders. "It's *my* fault," she states emphatically. In so doing, Patricia hammers the proverbial nail in the coffin of her self-esteem.

In therapy, Patricia came to understand how her pessimistic thinking was distorting her appraisal of her options. She began to entertain more optimistic interpretations, such as looking at her problems as temporary, specific to the way she and Stan interacted, and due at least as much to his personality flaws and shortcomings as to hers. As her pessimism cracked, life appeared less grim.

Patricia's pessimism also prevented her from becoming enraged with Stan. She feared becoming angry, equating the feeling with loss of control, and she viewed hostility as entirely "unacceptable behavior for a nice person." With the aid of therapy, she understood that by suppressing her anger at Stan and, instead, directing it at herself by assuming total blame for their problems, she was perpetuating two highly negative outcomes: First, she stayed depressed—immobilized, helpless, and hopeless; second, she could not communicate with Stan about their problems in a balanced, constructive way. As a consequence, together they could find no remedies to improve the emotional climate of their marriage.

The Giving Up/Given Up Complex

One great culprit consistently emerges in the research on how negative emotional states damage health: an attitude of hopeless, helpless resignation that is dubbed the "giving up/given up complex." More than any other, this mindset yields a despairing depression that is correlated with a myriad of serious, sometimes even fatal illnesses.[15]

But, does the diagnosis of illness create the attitude? Or does despair create the fertile ground in which the illness can then breed? The truth probably lies somewhere in between. Most important, though, the critical difference between patients who are able to prolong survival even when they have a terminal diagnosis, and those who succumb quickly, is that the former group simply does not give up, while the latter does.

In his best-selling books about the psychological components of healing, Dr. Bernie Siegel describes what he calls his "exceptional patients" who, in many cases, outlived the odds of their prognoses. These exceptional individuals maintained love, faith, hope, and the ability to forgive others in the face of frightening, painful illness.[16]

On the other hand, however, Siegel has known patients who did not fare as well. These other people seemed to abandon hope, to resign themselves to helplessness, and to lose contact with their faith. In effect, they were in the process of giving up or, sadly, had already given up. In fact, doctors have long known that without the will to live, patients quite often die.

Lethal Lovers and Learned Helplessness

During my years as a practicing clinician, I have met numerous patients who, like Patricia, bear the unmistakable imprint of their Lethal Lovers. The definitive clue lies in their description of relationships in which the net effect on them is the experience of learned helplessness. Invariably, they are depressed, suffer from impaired self-esteem, and feel out of control and ineffectual in their lives. Often, they display the deadly giving up/given up complex. Not surprisingly, then, they frequently suffer from physical ailments, most often related to immune system dysfunction.

Like Patricia, these patients describe lovers or mates who exercise almost total control over their fate. This means that the patients submit to and empower their partners to decide virtually everything for them—what they *do*, how they *look*, and, most important, how they *feel*. In other words, the partners' moods and actions entirely determine whether the patients are happy or sad, relaxed or nervous, calm or frightened.

Naturally, there are enormous underlying dependency needs and insecurities that predispose the patients to such relationships, just as their Lethal Lovers have excessive needs to dominate them. So one-sided and imbalanced is the control that, in the patients' experience, nothing they do matters to, or affects, their partners in any way. This, of course, is the necessary condition for learned helplessness.

Joanne, another victim of learned helplessness, had a great deal of sexual experience and confidence in her sexual adequacy and attractiveness prior to her affair with Marv. Joanne did not think of herself as particularly intelligent, nor did she pursue her education or a career. Instead, she counted on her good looks and sexy figure to attract the kind of man she wanted—"someone wealthy, powerful, brilliant, and strong."

At 28, Joanne met Marv, a 38-year-old self-made millionaire with a brash, controlling personality and highly articulate verbal skills. As Joanne liked to say, Marv "could talk his way out of anything and leave the other person thanking him." Shortly after they met, Joanne moved in with Marv. To solidify their relationship, she began working as Marv's personal assistant in his company.

At first, Joanne believed herself to be the luckiest woman in the world, with exactly the kind of man she had always wanted. In fact, she felt so fortunate that she harbored a nagging fear that her luck might change and Marv would leave her. As a result, she was willing to do just about anything Marv wanted in order to keep him.

Marv wanted a great deal. For example, he demanded that Joanne prove that she was open to new experiences and willing to take risks. The proof Marv wanted required her to attend sexual orgies with him, at which she was expected to seduce total strangers and invite Marv to watch or, at his discretion, to participate in "a threesome." This, he calmly explained, was necessary in order to sustain his sexual interest in her.

Despite her repugnance to the idea, Joanne was too fearful of losing Marv to protest. To satisfy Marv's desires, Joanne used alcohol and drugs so that she could force herself to "go to those parties and do what he wanted." However, after a few orgy episodes, Joanne begged Marv to stop going to the parties or at least to allow her to stay home. When she told him that she felt revolted and degraded by the behavior he demanded, Marv responded with an intense verbal attack. To punish Joanne, he withheld both affection and conversation until she relented and agreed, once again, to his aberrant sexual requests.

Marv dominated Joanne in other ways as well. He made all the decisions—from where and what they ate for dinner to when and how they had sex. Marv selected her clothes and determined the style of her hair. She read the books he told her to read and watched the television programs that he chose. In short, Joanne allowed Marv to exercise total control over every aspect of her life.

Despite her compliance with his every request, Marv was constantly critical. He told Joanne that she was "sexy but dumb" and that she didn't "have the brains to understand how to please him." These remarks terrified Joanne since she believed they signaled that Marv was about to end the relationship. And, although she was unhappy in several respects, Joanne had become too accustomed to Marv's affluence and fast-lane lifestyle to endure abandonment.

After two years of living with Marv, Joanne broached the subject of marriage and children. At first, Marv only laughed, insisting that Joanne "must be kidding." Then he launched into a monologue on how completely impossible it would be for him ever to marry a woman with Joanne's sexual history— particularly her participation in orgies. He dismissed as preposterous the notion that he would have children with anyone as "stupid and weak" as Joanne.

"How could you possibly take care of children?" he asked mockingly. "You can't even take care of yourself. I have to do everything for you, I have to make all your decisions. If I didn't give you a job, you wouldn't be working. You're not even an adult, so how could you think of being a mother?"

Joanne was devastated. She cried hysterically and asked Marv if he wanted her to leave. He adamantly denied any such thought.

"You're perfect for me, honey," he responded. "You're just a little screwed up, that's all. I'll talk to my doctor and get you some tranquilizers. You'll be okay. Just do what I say."

By the time Joanne came to see me three years later, she was teetering on the edge of suicide. Since she had accepted Marv's assessment of her personality as accurate, she felt hopeless, helpless, and fully to blame for all her problems.

She felt so ashamed and degraded by the aberrant sexual behavior Marv had continued to require that she agreed she was unfit for any other man or for motherhood. Joanne's dependence on Marv was so complete and her self-esteem so debased that she could not imagine exercising the alternative of leaving the relationship.

"Who would want me now?" she asked. "I always wanted to get married and have kids and now I've completely screwed up my life. I hate myself."

Joanne's was one of the most extreme cases of learned helplessness and domination that I have seen in my years of clinical practice.

I never saw Marv in therapy, nor did I wish to. Joanne's desperation was so acute that crisis intervention was required. She was briefly hospitalized (Marv was kept away); after just a few weeks, without his domination and without the dangerous drugs she had been taking, her mind cleared sufficiently for her to be receptive to the idea of going home to her family, who lived out of state. Thankfully, Joanne had loving parents who immediately came to her rescue.

By getting as far away from Marv as possible and with the help of a fine therapist in the city to which she moved, Joanne healed. At my last contact, she was engaged to marry "a nice, normal guy" and was looking forward to motherhood.

Learned Helplessness in Other Relationships

The chokehold of learned helplessness is not confined to relationships with Lethal Lovers. I have also witnessed its damaging effects in familial and work relationships.

Recall, for example, the case of Dan and his temperamental, controlling boss, Hank. Dan's relationship to Hank is remarkably equivalent to that of the dogs in the learned-helplessness experiments. As you will remember from the story, Dan receives phone calls at all times of the day and night whenever one of Hank's dysfunctional children or ex-wives presents another problem. Since Dan can exercise virtually no control over the negative events that affect him, his circumstances create a profound sense of futility and helplessness.

Moreover, Dan has internalized many of Hank's criticisms of

his personality over the many years of their association. As a consequence, his self-esteem is severely impaired and his perception of other career alternatives essentially foreclosed. Dan feels so deeply inadequate that he cannot imagine anyone else hiring him or any job that would meet his present level of financial compensation given his limited background. So, Dan is staying in his dependent and abusive relationship with Hank, while effectively giving up all hope that his life can be different or better.

Finally, there is the case of Ruth and her learned helplessness bred by her difficult, withholding mother. At age 25, Ruth was anxious, depressed, and suffering from a number of stress-related health problems including hair loss, skin disorders, irritable bowel syndrome, and temporal mandibular joint syndrome (TMJ).

Ruth had a good career as an attorney and a promising new relationship with a man. The bane of Ruth's existence was her mother, a negative, resentful person who had lost her husband prematurely and had taken out her frustration and loneliness on her only daughter. Instead of seeking a closer relationship, Ruth's mother seemed intent on driving an emotional wedge between them.

When her father died, Ruth grieved deeply. They had had a close, affectionate relationship that always had been the object of her mother's jealousy. Now, as an aging widow, her mother still felt rivalrous and competitive with Ruth concerning their respective opportunities to marry. Instead of offering encouragement and support when Ruth told her about a new man she was seeing, her mother manifested her jealousy by finding ways to inject negativity into Ruth's thinking.

"Why don't you keep looking around?" her mother would suggest when Ruth described a new man in her life. "This relationship probably won't work out, and it sounds to me like you could do a lot better."

Each time her mother responded in this typically negative, critical fashion, Ruth became upset. Despite years of experience with her mother's depressed behavior, Ruth maintained the belief that the reason for their lack of closeness was her failure as a daughter.

"I want to be close to my mom," Ruth would say. "I know she's unhappy and that she needs me. But I just don't know how to do it. No matter what I achieve, she's never proud of my accomplishments. She criticizes every boyfriend I've ever had and always tries to undermine my feelings toward them. My mother has a depressing effect on me, but I feel guilty for responding that way. It's all so confusing."

Ruth was flailing around emotionally with her mother, trying to find a solution to an insolvable problem. In fact, Ruth's mother had serious psychological problems of her own, but was unwilling to accompany Ruth for therapy sessions or to seek professional help herself.

Ruth's bond with her negative, punitive mother had created the conditions of learned helplessness: She felt that her attempts to please her mother were futile and that nothing she could do would gain her the close, accepting relationship that she desired. Moreover, since Ruth continually blamed herself for the problem, her self-esteem grew precarious while her need for her mother's unattainable approval intensified. Like other victims of learned helplessness, Ruth was caught in a vicious cycle of depression and rejection.

In therapy, Ruth learned to focus on alternative relationships from which she could receive approval and positive reinforcement. Once she was able to perceive that the reasons for her difficulties with her mother were at least partially due to her mother's negativity and not entirely to her own shortcomings as a daughter, Ruth could formulate a plan for relating to her mother differently.

She stopped telling her mother as much about the men she was dating, thereby removing the ammunition her mother had to use against her. Ruth learned to accept the limitations of her mother's capacity for intimacy and to appropriately lower her expectations of the relationship. Ruth's emotional needs for an accepting, loving mother remained unmet. However, she did learn to protect herself from the chronic feelings of helplessness, inadequacy, failure, and depression that her mother's behavior previously had induced. And, as the stress of her frustration decreased, Ruth's health conditions correspondingly improved.

Learned Helplessness: Victims and Perpetrators

One of the worst things that happens to victims of learned helplessness is precisely that they feel and function like victims. This means that they come to passively accept the role in which they have been placed or allowed themselves to be placed. As victims, they feel ashamed, helpless, depressed, out of control, and very low on self-esteem.

The underlying error in thinking that such victims make is that they are getting in life what they deserve. This belief derives from the equally erroneous assumption that "life is fair."

Victims of learned helplessness become pessimistic about life generally; ill (often with disorders of the immune system); unable to experience much pleasure in life (a prominent symptom of clinical depression); and devoid of self-confidence and self-esteem. Such damaged individuals stay in toxic relationships because they have given up hope that life can be different.

It is likely that people who become victims of learned helplessness have fairly low self-esteem in the first place. They may suffer from doubts about their attractiveness, competence, sexual adequacy, intelligence, and other key traits, which set them up as targets for their toxic partners. In addition, their dependent personalities make them all too willing to empower partners who have excessive needs to dominate and control others.

Another predisposing characteristic is a tendency toward rigid thinking. Certain unbending beliefs reinforce helplessness, such as, "Once I get married, I must always stay married no matter what," and "No problem is unsolvable if I just try hard enough." This kind of thinking causes the victim to dig a deeper and deeper psychological hole in a toxic relationship until the sunlight of hope can no longer be seen.

Ironically, the perpetrators of learned helplessness often are just as miserable as their victims. However, since they tend to be "externalizers"—blaming their problems on someone or something outside of them—they do not acknowledge any responsibility for the problems they help to create and, consequently, rarely seek therapeutic help.

Perpetrators of learned helplessness have a need to control and dominate others. Typically, they are frustrated, hostile people who demonstrate little insight into their behavior and motivations. Instead, they exploit other people, usually those closest to them. Finally, they usually lack the capacity to experience empathy.

Perpetrators often are not conscious of their malevolent actions. Nevertheless, their stubborn unwillingness even to examine the motivations for their behavior does not alter the fact that they indeed cause pain to others.

Who Survives Learned Helplessness?

People who escape learned helplessness do so by mustering the courage to change themselves from victims to survivors. Just how this process is activated varies from one individual to another. Often, the victim has a corrective experience that is sharply incongruous with the erroneous beliefs that he or she holds. Sometimes, that challenge comes from input given by someone outside the relationship—such as a therapist, friend, or co-worker. The incongruity between the outsider's affirming feedback and the victim's negative self-image strains the psychological shackles that have kept the person in a hurtful, damaging situation. For example, a male friend or co-worker might convince a self-effacing woman that she *is* attractive or exciting, contrary to her husband's perception.

Whatever activates the survivor response, its essence is *hope*. Once the pessimism is punctured and gives way to a more optimistic way of looking at problems—as *temporary*, *specific* to the situation, and *external*—the psychological and physical self-healing mechanisms are set in motion.

Survivors of learned helplessness usually experience what I call the "mental lightbulb" phenomenon. This catapults them out of the hurtful involvement by suddenly heightening their awareness of alternative ways to view their options. By learning to recognize the elements of learned helplessness, your mental lightbulb may be illuminated. Then, you will realize that the reasons for feeling depressed, helpless, or inadequate may well be due to the *relationship you are in* rather than to your inherent flaws or permanent deficiencies. With that shift of focus, you will see new possibilities that will stop your pain and unhappiness while opening opportunities for a healthier, fulfilling relationship.

12

The Big Chill

They met on holiday in the Caribbean. Maida was 28, gorgeous, and single; Brian was 42, handsome, wealthy, and recently divorced. Both said later that the first time they saw each other, they knew "this was it."

The romance exploded throughout the three weeks of what became an extended vacation. Neither could get enough of the other sexually. Their lovemaking was glorious. The last night of their trip, they proclaimed their love for each other and promised to do everything possible to find a way to be together. Then they tearfully parted, Brian to return to his Wall Street law practice and Maida to her modeling and acting career in Los Angeles.

After two months of long-distance telephone calls and biweekly trips across country, Brian proposed. Presenting Maida with a three-carat diamond, he implored her to give up her career, move to New York, and let him take care of her forever. The thought of other men ogling her beautiful body in magazines or kissing her in acting scenes, he explained, was simply intolerable for him. She found his possessiveness endearing and happily agreed to move to New York.

Maida moved into Brian's beautiful penthouse on the Upper East Side, complete with houseman, cook, and maid. Their wedding was small and elegant, followed by a ten-day deluxe honeymoon in London and Paris.

"The problems may have started during our honeymoon, I can't exactly recall," Maida told me. "I do know for sure that Brian changed when we came back to New York and resumed a normal life. He became very remote and distant from me. I'm a very physical person and I *need* a lot of physical affection—by that I mean cuddling and holding, not just sex.

"In fact," she continued, "my whole life as an adult woman, men have wanted to be with me for sex. Don't get me wrong, I love being sexual. But sometimes I just want to be held and comforted, without actually making love.

"I know I represent a sexual fantasy to a lot of guys, and that's the only way most of them relate to me. But I was sure that Brian would be different. He had been so warm and affectionate at first," Maida described. "But suddenly he seemed to be annoyed with my need for affection. He said that he didn't have time for hugs and kisses if it wasn't going to lead to sex. He told me my craving for affection was infantile. We continued to have sex—I think it was still good for him—but I never felt the same again."

When Brian withdrew his affection, Maida became increasingly frantic. During the six months of their ill-fated marriage, she lost twenty pounds and suffered from chronic stomach pains and bowel problems.

"I felt panicky all the time," Maida explained. "I didn't understand my feelings, except that Brian really had thrown me off balance. As my anxiety got worse, my need to be held and reassured became greater. But Brian only got angrier and angrier.

"Then his behavior started getting pretty crazy. He began drinking too much but he refused to admit it or get help. When he became verbally and sexually abusive, I knew I had to leave.

At that point, I was starved for affection, freaked out, and heartbroken. And my health was going down the tubes. Looking back on the whole nightmare, I'm glad I only stayed married six months. But it'll take me a long time to trust another guy again, I'll tell you that."

Cuddling and Health: The Power of Touch

Maida's story dramatically illustrates how denial of physical love and affection—as distinct from sex—can have profoundly negative consequences on health. In fact, the absence of touch, warmth, and affection can be almost as injurious to adults as to infants and children, and the damage applies equally to males and females.

Physiological as well as psychological injury occurs when infants and children are denied adequate physical contact, cuddling, and love. Evidence shows that dense lines on the bone X-rays of children (indicating periods of stunted or retarded growth) can be correlated with periods when physical love was actually insufficient.[17]

The "failure to thrive" syndrome is the label medical researchers ascribe to the phenomenon of infants who become severely underweight and undersized as a result of inadequate attention, cuddling, and love. Institutionally reared infants who receive food, clothing, and shelter but who nevertheless fail to thrive bear sad testimony to the fact that basic material necessities are not sufficient for normal development.

Without adequate cuddling, human babies do not grow up healthy; tragically, some do not grow up at all. Studies also show that premature infants who are given more emotional warmth and stroking develop better than do those who remain relatively love-deprived.[18]

The need for what is called *contact comfort*—a powerful psychological and physical drive in babies—originally was demonstrated in a now classic experiment that created two types of "substitute mothers" for baby rhesus monkeys: One was a cold wire structure that held a feeding bottle; the other was a warm, padded, constructed figure that provided physical comfort but no food.[19]

The baby monkeys were free to go to either of the two mothers. As expected, they went to the cold, wire mother for feeding. But when the babies were tired or afraid, they consistently chose the mother that provided contact comfort. Clearly, physical warmth was more emotionally satisfying than were mere sucking and feeding.

While there are few systematic studies on adults' need for contact comfort, a good deal of anecdotal clinical evidence—such as Maida's case and many others—demonstrates quite compellingly that adults, like children, need lots of tender loving care complete with cuddles, hugs, and other forms of warm physical contact.

There is intriguing anecdotal evidence showing that the blood pressure of adults can be lowered by providing them with a pet—a dog or cat—that they can stroke and cuddle. Elderly infirm residents of nursing homes have shown marked improvements in functioning—both physically and psychologically—with the benefit of periodic visits by young children. The surrogate grandchildren offer the elderly people not only a renewed sense of purpose but the physical comfort of spontaneously offered hugs and kisses.

The psychological correlates of physical touch, warmth, and affection include many of the positive emotions that are known to facilitate healing: love, security, relaxation, trust, and even faith. In contrast, deprivation of affection—in adults or children—can raise the level of toxic emotions such as anxiety, fear, frustration, and insecurity. Interestingly, the failure to thrive syndrome in infants—including weight/appetite loss, lassitude, and sleep disturbance—bears a number of resemblances to the syndrome of psychiatric depression in adults.

"Real Men" Don't Cuddle?

Although few men are as extreme as Brian, many deprive themselves of the health benefits of contact comfort achieved through nonsexual cuddling. Cultural conditioning seems the likely culprit.

From early in life, boys receive the cultural message that "real men don't cry," and that they shouldn't need or expect the same level of holding, cuddling, and other forms of physical attention from their parents as girls do. Moreover, boys are generally discouraged from expressing such "unmanly" emotions as fear, anxiety, and insecurity, which might elicit a tactile physical response.

Since as boys they received far less physical touch and cuddling from their parents than did girls, many men are quite uncomfortable with the admission that they, too, *need* hugs and cuddles; some cannot even feel or acknowledge that such a need exists. For a number of men, any form of physical closeness with a woman is confused with sexual foreplay. Therefore, if they comply with a request to cuddle from their wives or girlfriends, but are prohibited from continuing the experience to the point of sexual contact, they experience rejection, "teasing," or disappointment. Consequently, cuddling can become a conditioned source of frustration, resentment, and even hostility.

In a psychological sense, it is not only perfectly healthy for men to desire and initiate nonsexual or desexualized cuddling, it is protective of their physical health.

Displaced Affection

Jason was the unusual man who clearly knew that he needed and desired lots of physical warmth and tactile love from his wife. When they married in their midtwenties, Jason and Suzie were highly affectionate with each other, both inside and outside the bedroom.

In fact, Jason's need for contact comfort was exaggerated due to the fact that both his parents had been alcoholics. Consequently, his childhood needs for adequate, consistent love and warmth went sorely unmet. For Jason, as an adult, Suzie's warmth and comfortable physicality were enormously satisfying and meaningful. Indeed, he equated physical affection with genuine love far more than he equated it with sex.

To Jason, Suzie's tenderness and affection translated into deep feelings of emotional security, peacefulness, calm, safety, and comfort. Suzie provided the kind of nurturing that he had craved but never received from his dysfunctional mother. In a real sense, then, Suzie "mothered" Jason in many ways, including the cuddling and snuggling she encouraged and willingly provided.

When Suzie was 28, she gave birth to twins. Initially, Jason thought that he was prepared for the inevitable changes in their relationship that parenthood would necessitate. He understood that his wife's pregnancy and postpartum hormonal changes might produce some differences in her behavior.

But he was not prepared for the severe postpartum depression that Suzie suffered for nearly four months. During that difficult period, Suzie was almost totally unavailable to Jason and the twins both emotionally and physically. Not only was she completely uninterested in any sexual contact with Jason, but she was repelled by his attempts to cuddle and hold her.

With professional help and medication, Suzie recovered to a nearly normal level of daily functioning by the time the twins were about six months old. However, she remained physically distant from and cold to her husband. Jason felt left out in the emotional cold, bereft of the cuddling and snuggling that he needed so much. When he spoke to her about her coldness, Suzie's explanation was that she had "nothing left to give after giving it all to the babies."

Suzie felt guilty about being resentful and emotionally distant from the babies during the worst months of her depression. At considerable expense, Jason had even hired a live-in baby nurse, since Suzie was emotionally incapable of meeting the infants' needs. Once she was better, Suzie was determined to compensate—or overcompensate—for what she considered the unforgivable lack of love she had shown them earlier.

Consequently, Suzie threw herself into the role of the loving and affectionate mother in an excessive way. She tried to hold and cuddle the babies as much of each day as she could and insisted on bringing the twins into bed with her at night.

By the time the twins were ten months old, it was Jason's turn to develop a serious depression. He felt angry and resentful toward the babies for taking his mothering wife away from him, and he was frustrated and hostile toward Suzie for abandoning and rejecting him. Without the physical comfort of his marriage, Jason felt insecure, frightened, nervous, and out of control.

While Suzie apparently could channel her needs to give and receive affection to the babies, Jason was unable to do so. Periodically his frustration and anger would surface, but when he expressed his feelings to Suzie, her hostile retorts made him feel even more frustrated and guilty.

Suzie reminded him of how tenuous her emotional adjustment was and insisted that he refrain from putting any pressure on her to meet what she perceived as his selfish demands. She accused him of being a bad father for wanting to take the babies' mother away for himself.

By the twins' first birthday, the marriage was in deep trouble. Jason had started drinking heavily to anesthetize the pain he felt; Suzie was still too overwhelmed with motherhood and the demands of twins to address their marital and sexual issues, and she continued to ask Jason to give her "a little more time."

Time ran out when Jason was hospitalized with an acute bleeding ulcer. The psychiatrist who saw him in the hospital suggested that perhaps Jason, unconsciously, *had* to become ill in order to make Suzie recognize his needs to be loved and nurtured.

Obviously, Jason and Suzie's case involves a number of complex issues. In some respects, though, it is an extreme variation of the normal adjustments and jealousies many new fathers feel when their wives become mothers. In other respects, of course, it resonates around much deeper psychological problems in both parents.

The story is important here because it boldly illustrates how vital a role physical affection, warmth, and nurturance play in the maintenance of marriages, as well as the physical and mental health of adults. The case serves as an important reminder that while babies and children do require lots of love and cuddling, they also need to *see and feel* plenty of physical love and affection between their parents.

Sexual Problems and Health

For a great many adults, the need for simple contact comfort becomes clouded by the murky waters of sex. When, for example, does cuddling stop and foreplay begin? Must "loving" or "romantic" sex always include tenderness, warmth, and lots of tactile stroking? Can't "healthy" lovemaking sometimes just be good old-fashioned genital sex without all the touchy-feely stuff? Who has the rule book?

In fact, these questions and myriad others boil down to individual preferences, desires, and compatibilities, all of which require three things: communication, communication, and communication.

Clinical experience and anecdotal evidence suggest some gender differences in sexual preferences, although such generalizations are somewhat perilous. Women, for example, seem to want and/or need more contact comfort as a precursor to sex than do men; but neither men nor women always *mean* for cuddling to be interpreted as a prelude or demand for sex.

The very presence of sex—or even its possibility—as a factor in a relationship often interferes with getting contact-comfort needs adequately satisfied. In part, this is because of the physical overlap between cuddling and more overtly sexual behavior. Tensions, resentments, and other unresolved issues that arise out of troubled sexual relationships also take their toll; affection and warmth are often withheld in response to such underlying psychological currents.

Sexual problems do not pose health threats merely because they interfere with the healing benefits of touch and physical-contact comfort. In a very real sense, you bare your psyche and soul as well as your body when you enter the realm of sexual love in an intimate relationship.

An unsatisfying or dysfunctional sexual relationship can strike at the very core of your self-concept—how you think and feel about yourself as a person. If you are not desired sexually by someone you love and desire, for example, you may wind up feeling wholly unworthy and unlovable. Or, if you do not perform satisfactorily, you may feel profoundly inadequate.

Problematic sexual relationships produce many other complex feelings. The pernicious thing about sexual dysfunctions is that the feelings they *produce* are often the very *causes* of the problems in the first place. While most of the negative emotions associated with sexual difficulties—such as depression, stress, frustration, or low self-esteem—pose potential health threats, there are three, in particular, that merit special attention because of the vicious, escalating cycles they produce: *anxiety*, *hostility*, and *fear of loss of control*.

Anxiety and Sexual Dysfunction

By far, the emotion most closely associated with disorders or dysfunctions in sexual performance is *anxiety*. If there ever were a contest for the emotion most likely to produce self-fulfilling prophecies, this one is it. The man who feels very anxious about his ability to perform well in bed is most likely to develop erectile difficulties or premature ejaculation; the woman who worries and frets over whether she will be orgasmic is least likely to reach the orgasm she desires.

Anxiety does not have to be specifically focused on sexual performance issues in order to interfere with them. An individual who is highly anxious or stressed because of problems unrelated to sex is still more likely to develop sexual dysfunction problems than is a less anxious person.

Sexual dysfunctions caused by anxiety can be treated quite successfully with behavior modification methods *provided* that both partners are amenable to working together, with a non-judgmental attitude, to improve their relationship. On the other hand, some of the most intractable sexual problems occur when one partner reacts to the dysfunction of the other in ways that exacerbate the anxiety and create the vicious chicken-and-egg cycle.

Alice and Mark, for example, had been married for ten years when he began to suffer erectile problems. In the preceding year, Alice had become bored as a full-time housewife and mother and had returned to her professional career as a CPA.

Initially, Mark had been supportive of her return to work, especially since his income as a stockbroker had declined sharply in recent years. But when Alice started working very long hours and traveling a lot, Mark started worrying.

He had always had quite mixed feelings about professional women, finding himself attracted to them but psychologically threatened at the same time. Mark became distracted at work as he wondered whether the men in Alice's office were ogling her or flirting with her as the men in his office did with the women brokers. He knew for a certainty that two married women in his office were having affairs with men who worked there.

The more Alice worked, the less secure Mark became. To add to the problem, within a year of her return to work, Alice was earning nearly double Mark's salary.

"She really doesn't need me much anymore," Mark said to me. "If she left me, she could easily support herself and the kids. Alice is a very attractive woman. It won't take her much time before she hooks up with one of her wealthy male clients . . . unless she already has."

Mark loved his wife and anguished deeply over the thought of losing her. He wanted and needed to show her his love sexually. So, when he couldn't achieve an erection one night, he panicked. At first, Alice reacted calmly. She told him not to worry and rolled over and went to sleep. But Mark stared at the ceiling half the night, thinking about the implications of becoming impotent. As the weeks went by, the sexual problems worsened. Mark was unable to achieve an erection. Predictably, the more anxious he felt about himself and about losing Alice, the less able he was to function sexually.

Then, after more than three months of sexual problems, Mark's anxiety took a new turn. Whereas initially he had been solicitous of Alice in an attempt to compensate for his inadequacy in the bedroom, he now became irritable and critical of her. Mark didn't like feeling so insecure about his wife and he began openly resenting her for going back to work. He blamed Alice for creating the deep concern and anxiety that made him feel so uncomfortable.

He blamed her also for his sexual problems. "Maybe if you were home more of the time like a real wife, I'd be more turned on to you," he would say defensively. Or, "Did you ever think that maybe you've become so damn aggressive as a career woman that you forgot how to turn me on in bed?"

Mark's comments wounded Alice deeply. She realized that Mark was stressed and preoccupied, but she had never dreamed that the husband who had loved and cherished her would "turn off," as he had suggested, just because she went back to work.

Alice agreed to cut back on her hours and to "try more things in bed to turn Mark on." Now, Alice was as anxious about Mark's erections as he was, since in her mind his sexual problems had come to reflect *her* inadequacy as a woman.

Over the course of nine months, Mark was able to achieve and maintain an erection only twice. On those occasions, he ejaculated almost immediately. Both Mark's and Alice's sexual frustrations were mounting.

When Alice finally suggested that they consult a sex therapist, Mark became enraged. Again, he lashed out and blamed her for losing her femininity and for trying to make him "feel like a eunuch."

Alice's sense of outrage at being blamed and unfairly treated now surfaced. It was her turn to attack back. In the heat of anger, she accused Mark of being "a sexist."

"You're such a flop as a man," she lashed out, "you can only be turned on to a woman that you feel superior to. When I was at home and not earning a dime, you felt like a big man. Now that I make nearly twice what you do, you can't function. You make me sick."

Mark and Alice had become Lethal Lovers. The toxic cycle of stress and sexual dysfunction had escalated to the point where it threatened their marriage and their respective emotional and physical health. They had allowed potent psychological poisons—hostility, frustration, and anxiety—to seep into their bedroom and contaminate their relationship.

Hostility and Sexual Dysfunction

A positive, gratifying sexual relationship provides continual opportunities for reducing stress and tension, satisfying contact comfort needs, validating self-worth, and expressing love. Thus, it also operates to thwart or counteract hostility. On the other hand, a troubled sexual relationship frustrates the gratification of these important needs. As a consequence, toxic *hostility* can become inextricably tangled in the cycle of sexual dysfunction and negative emotions.

Trouble in the bedroom often produces a dangerous spillover of anger, resentment, and hostility into the whole relationship. Conversely, both open and covert hostility in the relationship frequently create or exacerbate sexual problems of all kinds.

Because effective sexual functioning requires at least a moderate degree of relaxation, it is easily disrupted when the emotional atmosphere is laden with anger and tension. Like anxiety, hostility is related to numerous forms of sexual dysfunction, most closely to retarded ejaculation, inhibition of sexual desire, and, in women, inability to achieve orgasm.

When one or both partners misuse sex to coerce or punish the other, to manipulate, or to retaliate, hostility is the predictable result. Sexual gratification is a primal and intense need. To play with such a basic drive by intentionally withholding sex from your partner until certain conditions are met—such as gifts, favors, or remorse—is indeed to play with emotional fire. And once that angry blaze ignites, it is difficult to extinguish, remaining instead on a perennial slow burn.

When hostility is associated with the frustration of sexual needs in a relationship, it can trigger a domino effect, setting off a dangerous sequence of other toxic emotions. In this sense, hostility can breed cynicism, distrust, jealousy, resentment, and even hatred toward the partner. These known cardiac poisons pose significant threats to physical health while serving to perpetuate the vicious cycle of sexual problems/frustration/hostility/more sexual problems.

Fear of Loss of Control and Sexual Dysfunction

The third toxic emotion that both creates and results from sexual problems is *fear of loss of control.* Many cases of orgasmic dysfunction, in both women and men, are reflective of this concern.

Max and Sally, for example, had been strongly attracted to each other for years before they got together sexually. They met at a medical convention as the respective spouses of two physician colleagues. Both could recall being "completely turned on" when they were first introduced.

"In fact," Sally explained to me, "I was actually alarmed when I found out that Max and his wife lived in the same neighborhood as we did. I remember thinking how magnetic the chemistry was between us and what kind of trouble we might get into if we ever found ourselves alone together.

"Everyone else thought it was the two doctors—my husband and Max's wife—that had so much in common. What they had in common was how boring they both were. The truth was that Max and I were overwhelmingly drawn to each other, and neither of us was happily married.

"I certainly didn't get divorced in order to be with Max," Sally continued. "I had been thinking about leaving my husband long before Max and I ever met. But I won't deny that the fantasy of someday being with Max was in my head. Max stayed married to his wife for another year after I left my husband. As a matter of fact, Max and I hardly saw each other during that year, although we talked periodically by phone.

"I remember how mixed my feelings were when Max told me that he and his wife had split up. I was excited about the possibility of becoming more than just friends. But, at the same time, I was incredibly anxious.

"We started dating about three months after Max and his wife separated. Right from the first, I was never able to reach an orgasm with Max. Believe me, he's a fine lover; that wasn't the problem. And, like I said, I was *very* attracted to him, as he was to me.

"The problem," Sally went on, "was that I was *overly* attracted to Max. I mean, I used to stay up at night thinking about how I'd feel if I lost him to another woman. When I met Max, he was married but he sure responded to me. He's a very seductive and charming man.

"All I could think about was how to protect myself from getting hurt. I rationalized that I just wanted him as a friend and didn't want to mess everything up by falling in love. But I *was* in love with him. I just never had the guts to go with my feelings.

"So," Sally sighed, "I suppose I wound up creating what I was most afraid of—losing him. This sexual thing—my being unable to have an orgasm with him—started to drive him nuts. And it confused me because I had been orgasmic with nearly every other man I'd ever slept with. Max interpreted my lack of responsiveness (that's what he called it) as meaning that I didn't find him attractive or good enough in bed. He told me that he'd had years of sexual frustration with his ex-wife and that he couldn't bear to repeat that pain again.

"It got to be such an enormous pressure on me that there was simply no way that I could relax enough to even come close to an orgasm. The more uptight I got, the more frustrated he got. We started fighting more and more. After a few months, I broke off the relationship, telling him we weren't meant to be lovers and that we should just stay friends. What I really felt was that I wasn't good enough for him and that I knew he'd leave me."

Paradoxically, the root cause of Sally's inability to achieve orgasm with Max was the sheer intensity of feelings that he evoked in her. This intensity created a high degree of anxiety coupled with a strong fear of abandonment.

In fact, Sally's deeper fear was of losing control of herself. Before Max, all of Sally's relationships with men (including with her ex-husband) had one thing in common: The men felt more strongly for her than she did for them. This asymmetry was reassuring and comforting for her at first, but eventually the boredom and lack of passion on her end caused her to break off the relationships.

Unlike Max, Sally's prior boyfriends and husband had passive, unassertive personalities. Because Sally's feelings for these other men had been muted, she approached sex largely from a technical, nearly mechanical standpoint. Orgasms, in this context, were pleasurable and unthreatening; she was not shy about telling her lovers where and how to move or touch her so that the stimulation would be sufficient. This direction allowed her to reach orgasm while retaining the sense that she was in control.

With Max, however, Sally felt very much out of control. He was good-looking, smart, charming, and very assertive. In bed, he neither required nor welcomed directions. Being with Max physically evoked feelings she had never had—feelings that threatened to completely overwhelm her. In this context, giving up enough control to permit an orgasm was too threatening for Sally to handle.

Sally and Max gave their relationship another chance nearly two years after their first parting. During that interim time, however, Sally suffered depression and recurrent viral infections from which she became fatigued and debilitated.

The extent to which Sally internalized blame for the failure of their relationship was rivaled only by Max's self-punitive anger. On his part, Max continually faulted himself for not being more patient and understanding with Sally.

151

Fear of loss of control also can interfere with male orgasmic function. Retarded ejaculation, for example, occurs when orgasm and ejaculation are so prolonged (or inhibited altogether) as to cause discomfort or pain to both partners. Naturally, tension, frustration, and disappointment for both partners result from the man's inability to achieve ejaculatory release.

Retarded ejaculation generally is regarded as more difficult to treat than any other sexual dysfunction. Since it usually generates so much stress and so many toxic emotions, its occurrence in a relationship potentially endangers the health of both partners. And, the problem centers principally around the issue of control and fear of losing control.

Hugs, Sex, and Health

Just as body and mind cannot be separated when it comes to understanding the causes of illness, the physical and emotional sides of love relationships are inextricably intertwined. When the emotional climate of a relationship is warm and loving, positive, health-promoting emotions are expressed, through verbalizations, physical warmth, and gratifying sexual love. In contrast, when a relationship is strained by negative emotions, the withdrawal of affection and the frustration of sexual needs mirror and exacerbate the psychological poisons such feelings produce.

13

Fatal Personalities

For several years, I have conducted "PMMS" workshops. The letters stand for: People Make Me Sick.

The workshops' purpose is to help participants cope with the stress produced by the most difficult, aggravating people in their lives—people who upset them so much that illness, literally, has resulted.

The stories that are shared in these workshops give a dimension of frightening reality to those common figures of speech such as, "He's breaking my heart," "She's going to give me a stroke," "These kids are giving me ulcers," and, "That guy'll be the death of me." The participants' tales bring vividly to life why Dr. Hans Selye considered *interpersonal stress*—the stress to a person caused by the behavior of another—the most damaging and potentially lethal of all.[20]

The PMMS discussions cover the gamut of relationships: spouses, lovers, co-workers, bosses, subordinates, children, parents, friends, or anyone else who—as one participant succinctly put it—aggravates the life out of other people. Yet, despite the wide range of relationships discussed, four basic types of "difficult others" are described most frequently: (1) narcissistic personalities, (2) borderline personalities, (3) passive-aggressive personalities, and (4) addicts.

The first three types are psychiatric "personality disorders." This official designation is given to people who display certain enduring patterns of traits and behavior that:

- are rigid and inflexible
- severely damage an individual's social relationships
- severely disrupt an individual's ability to function at work
- cause considerable personal distress for the individual[21]

The clinical diagnosis of a personality disorder depends primarily on whether the patient has created disturbances in most or all relationships throughout his or her life. However, there is no official designation for the people—like those who attend the PMMS workshops—who become emotionally or physically ill as a result of being in a disturbed, close relationship with someone who has a personality disorder.

PMMS participants are usually diagnosed with symptoms that stress produces—such as depression, ulcers, anxiety, cardiovascular disease, drug or alcohol abuse, eating disorders, and so forth. However, these labels fail to convey that the symptoms have resulted, in large measure, from the stress inflicted on them by other people. Perhaps a new classification system should be developed with designations such as, "depression caused by being in love with a narcissistic man"; or, "heart disease aggravated by a wife with a borderline personality disorder."

The behavior of people who have personality disorders and addictions is typically so provocative that it tends to dominate and control relationships. This strong commonality among PMMS participants creates the sense that they all operate in a purely *reactive* mode when it comes to dealing with the difficult people in their lives. In this sense, many PMMS people strongly identify with the designation "codependent personality." The toxic feelings of loss of control and helplessness are common consequences.

Fatal Personality #1: The Narcissist

"I didn't grasp what he was all about until I got sick," Barbara, a PMMS member, told the others in the group about her ex-fiancé, Don. "Looking back, I know that the stress of my relationship with him probably had a lot to do with my getting cancer in the first place. But when my doctor told me to get away from Don if I wanted to have a fair shot at surviving, I realized just how damaging this guy was to me.

"I was thirty-five, divorced with two kids, when Don and I were introduced by a mutual friend," Barbara explained. "I thought he was the most exciting man I'd ever known. He was intelligent, good-looking, and very romantic. The thing I didn't realize was that he was more excited about himself than I was. He thought he was brilliant, gorgeous, and the greatest prize any woman could hope for. Don and I were both in love with the same person: Don.

"Don said he loved the fact that I was both a successful attorney and a feminine, attractive woman. He told me that most women weren't smart and special enough to understand someone like him; or, if they were intelligent, they weren't pretty or sophisticated enough for a man with his looks and social position.

"I was relieved that he wasn't threatened by me like a lot of men seem to be. My perception was that he was very self-confident and extremely successful. Much later, though, I found out how much he exaggerated things like his business deals, his importance in his industry, even his bank account. By then I was in love with him, and I rationalized that he had only wanted to impress me when we met.

"I remember one night, after we came home from a party that a friend of mine had given, I asked him why he had told people things about himself that weren't true," Barbara recalled. "It wasn't the first time he'd done something like that.

155

Don always needs to be the center of attention. He can be very charming and he just eats it up when people are impressed and compliment him. So he gets carried away to the point, frankly, of lying.

"But when I told him that I didn't like the fact that he invented stories, especially with my friends, he became icy. He told me I was too small-minded and that he had to do something to entertain himself since my friends weren't up to his caliber. I was appalled.

"There were lots of other problems in the relationship," Barbara continued. "Basically, he exhausted me physically and emotionally. He simply *expected* me to be there for him, even if my kids needed me or if I was tired. It didn't matter to him. If he had arranged a dinner with business associates, I was expected to be there and to look great—no matter what kind of day I'd had. And of course, I was never, *never* to outshine him. That would enrage him.

"I kept thinking that when we got married and he felt more secure with me, he'd stop doing some of the things that bothered me. Then I was diagnosed with breast cancer. I was lucky that they caught it early and I didn't have to have a radical mastectomy. But I did need radiation and chemotherapy. It was the most frightening thing that ever happened to me. I tried to tell Don that I needed to be in the best frame of mind possible.

"He told me that it was a good thing I hadn't been totally 'deformed' since he wouldn't have been able to deal with that," Barbara recounted. "Then, he let it be known that the chemotherapy was really annoying *him* because I was nauseated and ill for a few days after each treatment and wasn't available to go with him to parties or dinners.

"When I was in the hospital, after the surgery, he seemed to be jealous that I had so many friends and relatives come to visit. Don would try to get the attention off me and onto him.

"The final straw came when he told me that he wanted to postpone our wedding until my doctor had a better idea of my prognosis," Barbara concluded. "The incredible thing is that he didn't even realize how awful that was to say to me. In fact, when I criticized him for being so insensitive, he went berserk—yelling and screaming that all I thought about was myself and my illness instead of about what was best for him.

"That finished the relationship as far as I was concerned. But I went through six months of hell—between him and the cancer—before I figured out that *he* was a cancer in my life emotionally. I really believe that if I had married him, I wouldn't have lived very long."

Barbara's experience with Don captures the essence of narcissism and its impact on others. People with narcissistic personality disorders have a grandiose sense of self-importance that is often revealed by a tendency to exaggerate their talents and/or accomplishments, especially with the intention of receiving attention and notice for being a "special" person. The narcissist believes that his or her problems are unique and therefore can be understood only by other special people.

Narcissists mask their low self-esteem and feelings of unworthiness with grandiose behavior and fantasies. Their fragile self-esteem promotes a drive for constant attention and admiration. This craving for praise and compliments is coupled with an intolerance for criticism and a hypersensitivity to what others think of him or her. In the face of criticism, the narcissist generally responds with a display either of cool indifference or marked rage.

Narcissists' interpersonal relationships are invariably disturbed, principally due to a complete lack of empathy: The narcissist is unable to recognize or identify with how other people feel.

In romantic relationships, the narcissist's partner is not treated as a person with his or her own feelings and needs; rather, the partner is treated as an *object* whose purpose is solely to bolster the narcissist's self-esteem. Other people are frequently exploited, since the narcissist relates to virtually everyone in terms of how his or her own ends may be served.

157

Being in an intimate relationship with a narcissistic personality is usually a confusing, frustrating, disillusioning, depersonalizing, enraging, and tremendously stressful experience, which can seriously harm your health and dangerously interfere with your ability to recover from illness.

Fatal Personality #2: The Borderline

"When I started to date Suzanne, I'd say I was a pretty well-adjusted guy," Matt told the PMMS group. "As a matter of fact, I used to wonder if I was *too* 'normal' to be interesting enough for Suzanne. But, by the end of our relationship, there wasn't much about me that *was* normal: I was a total physical and emotional mess.

"My asthma and allergies—which had been under control for many years—seriously flared up as a result of all the stress. I also developed something called 'cluster headaches,' which are unbelievably painful and also related to stress and allergies.

"After a year with Suzanne, I was very nervous all the time. Her personality and mood can change like the weather. She could be in a great mood when I spoke to her on the telephone in the afternoon, and then by the time I'd pick her up for dinner a few hours later, she could be incredibly depressed. Or she could get angry—*really* angry—at the drop of a hat.

"For the first three months of our relationship, I was head over heels in love. She seemed like the woman of my dreams.

"I remember the first time that I thought her behavior was peculiar. We had been invited to a formal party that my boss was hosting for a charity. When I picked her up, I told her that she looked terrific. Then, just as we were about to leave her house, she looked at herself in the mirror and suddenly became very upset. She threw her purse against the wall and insisted that she had to change clothes. I tried to tell her that I loved how she looked, but she said I didn't know anything about how women should dress and that I was lying just so we wouldn't be late.

"Anyway," Matt went on, "we were about an hour late to

the party because she not only changed her dress but completely redid her hairstyle, too. And when she finally agreed to leave the house she still wasn't satisfied. All the way to the party she was surly and ill-tempered. But the minute we walked into the party, her mood completely changed. She became charming, vivacious, and lighthearted. I remember thinking how strange it was that she could turn her mood on and off like a switch.

"But none of her behavior turned me off. I was thoroughly in love. She said that she loved me, too—that she had never met anyone like me; that I was so 'anchored' and 'stabilizing' and that my values were so 'fine.' She thought I would make a great stepfather to her two teenaged daughters. By the way, Suzanne had been married three times before—the daughters were from two different fathers—and she hadn't maintained any connection or visitation arrangements with any of her ex-husbands.

"We talked about getting married after we had been seeing each other for just three months. I got along great with the two girls and they were genuinely excited.

"Then, the *really* crazy-making stuff started. A few days after we had told the girls about our marriage plans, Suzanne canceled a date with me. She said she needed some 'space' and that I was 'crowding' her by rushing the decision to marry. She told me that because I had never been married, I didn't know enough to realize what I was taking on. In retrospect, I can honestly say that she was right about that.

"I didn't see her for nearly a week," Matt recalled, "because she kept making excuses. One night, her nineteen-year-old daughter, Jessica, called and asked me to come over to help her study for her college math exam. When I got there, Suzanne wasn't home. Jessica said she wanted to talk with me before getting down to the math problems.

"I remember that conversation vividly because it spooked me. Jessica asked me—no, she begged me—to convince her mother to get professional help. She told me that her mother had destroyed her three marriages and, in her words, driven

159

her own father (husband #2) 'practically over the edge.' Jessica, incidentally, is a very high-strung girl herself.

"That night, she told me things about Suzanne that really made me worry," Matt continued. "She said that her mother had tried to slit her wrists twice—each time after the breakup of a relationship with a man—but that neither attempt had truly been intended to succeed. Suzanne had made only surface scratches and minor cuts on her wrists. The real purpose was to get attention rather than to inflict actual harm. Jessica also told me that her mother had gone through a few episodes of binge drinking.

"All of this was quite shocking and disturbing to me, and I wasn't even sure who to believe—Jessica or her mother. Jessica said that she loved her mom a lot and hoped that I would make a difference.

"When Suzanne came home later that evening and found me there, she became furious," Matt recalled. "She accused me of spying on her and told me that I wasn't the kind of man that she wanted to marry. Then she grabbed Jessica by the shoulders and shook her pretty violently. She screamed at Jessica, accusing her of making a pass at me! It was just crazy. As of that night, Suzanne didn't seem so irresistible anymore.

"Suzanne said incredibly hurtful things to both me and Jessica. She threw me out of the house, tellling me to go away and stay away. She said she had only been fooling herself into thinking that she could be happy with a 'weakling' like me.

"And I stayed away. Frankly, by this time I was fairly shaken up by Suzanne's behavior and by what Jessica had said. That night, in fact, I had a major asthma attack—my neighbor had to take me to the emergency room.

"But our separation lasted only for a week," Matt went on. "Suzanne called me and apologized profusely. She attributed her behavior to 'bad PMS' and made all kinds of proclamations of her undying love for me and said that she had been 'temporarily insane.' She told me that when she gets like that, I should 'take charge and slap her if necessary.'

"Our reconciliation lasted only about a month. During that

time, I saw more of her moodiness and fits of temper—mostly directed at her daughters. But I was still in love with her.

"Then, it happened again." Matt sighed. "We were on our way to a movie one night and she suddenly flipped out in the car. She said my driving made her crazy because I was so 'wimpy' about letting people pass me and push me around on the road. Then she started crying and yelling, saying that it was over between us and that I should take her home and get out of her life.

"I dropped her off and went home. One of those cluster headaches came on me and the pattern was starting to become clear. I made my mind up to get out of the relationship even though a big part of me wanted her back.

"The best thing that I did," Matt said, "was to start going out with other women. Predictably, Suzanne called me after we had been apart for a month. Once again, she said all the right things: that she loved me; that I represented the kind of man and the values that she wanted in her life; that she had been nuts to break up with me but that she had just been frightened about getting married; and so on.

"But this time I wasn't so easily manipulated. In fact, I was pretty interested in one of the women I'd been seeing, and Suzanne's erratic behavior seemed unattractive. When I told her I wasn't prepared to get back together, the *really* bizarre stuff started.

"First, she sent about twenty floral arrangements to my office with mushy love notes on each. When I didn't call her to acknowledge the extravagant gesture, she got upset. She must have called my answering machine that night at least ten times. I didn't want to speak to her so I didn't pick up the phone. At first, the messages were kind of cute and flirtatious. But, after about four calls, she became irate.

"On some messages, she was furious—yelling and swearing, calling the woman that she assumed was in my house all kinds of terrible names. Then, on other calls, she was hysterically sobbing, blaming herself for being so 'stupid' and telling me that she wouldn't blame me a bit if I came over and beat her up. The more she carried on, the more turned off I got.

"The next day, I called to say that I thought we should stay apart from each other for a while. She really lost control—sobbing and screaming—and said that if she lost me she'd kill herself. She begged me just to get together so we could talk things out. I gave in and agreed to see her that night.

"When I drove up to her house," Matt continued, "I was expecting to see a distraught woman. I was trying to think of how to handle her in case she tried to hurt herself. But when she answered the door, she was the picture of self-control, dressed very elegantly in sexy lounging pajamas. And she had changed the color of her hair from blond to red. I was shocked.

"Right away she tried to hug and kiss me. When I moved back and said that I didn't feel comfortable being physical with her, she flipped out again. This time she accused me of 'abandoning' her. She kept telling me to hit her and demanded to know what it was that I wanted her to do to make things up to me. It was all terribly dramatic and wildly inappropriate.

"The whole display made me so nervous that I had an asthma attack then and there. Her reaction was the last straw. She had been hysterically sobbing just a moment before my wheezing started. Suddenly she just turned off the crying and attacked me verbally in an intensely angry way. She said I was just trying to get attention and to make her feel sorry for me. And she said the asthma convinced her that she had been right all along—that I wasn't the kind of guy for her to marry.

"She demanded that I leave the house, in spite of the fact that I still was having a lot of trouble breathing," Matt concluded. "I knew then that I needed to get as far away from that woman as possible. It's taken me a few months in therapy to come to terms with all this—to understand what's wrong with Suzanne and to figure out some of my reactions.

"Incidentally," Matt added, "Suzanne continued for several months to call me periodically and suggest that we get back together. But I've stood my ground."

* * *

162

Matt's story illustrates some of the physical and psychological consequences of being on the "receiving end" of a borderline personality disorder. Patients with this disorder—usually more common in women—generally comprise the most intractable and frustrating group in any therapist's practice. Usually, however, it is the individuals involved with borderlines who present themselves for therapy rather than those who themselves suffer from the disorder.

The term *borderline* is largely a misnomer in that it does not mean that the individual is "on the border" of anything. Many people who hear the term assume it to refer to someone who is almost, but not quite, psychotic; or just on the "edge" of serious mental illness.

Rather, people with a borderline personality disorder have a pattern of instability in their self-image, moods, and interpersonal relationships.

As evidenced by Suzanne's treatment of Matt, the borderline's interpersonal relationships are generally very intense, unstable, and they can swing wildly between extremes of idealization ("You're the most wonderful man I've ever met") and devaluation ("You're the weakest and most inadequate person I've ever known"). These people thrive on all of the drama and chaos that are the typical course of their relationships.

They find it extremely difficult to tolerate being alone and may go to frantic lengths to avoid or forestall real or imagined abandonment. Their intolerance of being alone is due in part to a marked disturbance in their sense of identity. This disturbance is often revealed in uncertainty or crises over such issues as self-image, sexual orientation, long-term goals or choice of careers, which types of lovers or friends to have, or which values to embrace and hold. Their mood may change from normal to depression, irritability, or anxiety in a moment's time; the altered state may then last for only a few hours until yet another shift occurs. Moreover, these sufferers are quite prone to outbursts of intense anger over which they seem to lack control. In addition, impulsive behavior such as spending sprees, drinking binges, overeating, reckless driving, promiscuous sex, or even shoplifting is common.

In more extreme cases, suicidal gestures—such as Suzanne's wrist-scratching—take place, usually designed to manipulate others or to express intense anger.

For Matt, and others like him who find themselves involved with a borderline personality, toxic emotions become the predominant experience in the relationship. Chronic uncertainty, anxiety, frustration, and hostility characterize the reactions of those who become the objects of the borderline's disruptive behavior.

There are two particular features of borderline behavior that warrant special mention. The first is the emotional extortion to which they frequently subject their partners. When Suzanne, for example, threatened to kill herself unless Matt agreed not to abandon her, she was exerting highly coercive control. Essentially, her modus operandi was blackmail: "You do what *I* want or else I will hurt myself and you will be responsible."

As a clinician, I have treated many anguished husbands and boyfriends (and an occasional wife or girlfriend) over the years who have been victimized by the extortional demands of their borderline partners. The dangerous aspect of this blackmailing behavior is that every time the partner relents and gives in to the borderline's coercive demands, he or she strongly reinforces the manipulative action. Clearly, however, it is very difficult to deny the demands, given the nature of the threats.

Nevertheless, there is only one way to respond to blackmail and that is to defy it. Naturally, suicidal threats or gestures must be taken seriously and dealt with appropriately by taking prompt steps to place the individual in the care of competent professionals. But, once a victim of extortion submits to demands—however understandable, given the extreme nature of the threats—his or her own freedom will be lost and the shackles of coercive control will only tighten.

The second feature to note about borderlines is the provocation of violence. In the case of Suzanne and Matt, several times she exhorted him to beat her up as a way of punishing her. Fortunately, Matt was a sufficiently controlled person to resist the provocation and to recognize the behavior as abnormal.

However, in many borderline relationships, the provocation to violence is even more extreme and the self-control of the partner is not as solid as Matt's. The continual frustration that is created by the borderline's erratic mood and behavior primes the pump of hostility. In their impulsive anger, borderlines often resort to physical attack or abuse as a way to act out hostility.

Once the relationship takes a dangerous turn to physical violence, a cycle of guilt, remorse, further provocation, and further violence can take hold. Now, the threat to physical survival becomes far more immediate than that caused just by emotional toxins.

Fatal Personality #3: The Passive-Aggressive Personality

Since Meg was promoted to director of marketing in her company, she had suffered from an array of physical problems including recurrent viruses, sinus infections, hives and rashes, and other ailments that her doctor labeled as "stress related." While Meg agreed with the doctor's assessment, she took exception to his analysis of the source of her stress.

"My doctor—a man—keeps telling me that I'm overly ambitious and that the stress of my job responsibilities is the cause of my physical problems," Meg told the PMMS group. "But I just don't agree. I *am* ambitious and I think that's just fine. I *want* to be that way. I bet he doesn't tell his male patients that they're overly ambitious; he just says they're 'successful.' It's maddening.

"I'll admit that a lot of my stress comes from problems at work," Meg continued, "and the biggest problem I have is a guy named Norm. Just about every night of the week I go home aggravated and frustrated over something Norm has or, more accurately, has not done.

"Norm is in charge of all special promotions that my department puts on," Meg explained. "He's been with the company for a few years longer than I have, and I know he was very upset when I got the directorship instead of him. I should add that Norm is in what we call a 'protected position'—his uncle is the CEO of the company. So there's little chance of Norm losing his job.

"He knows that the next step for me, if I succeed in this position, is assistant vice president. I'd be the first woman in the company to make it to that level and, I admit, I really *do* want it.

"My job performance is evaluated on the basis of what my department, as a whole, accomplishes. The higher-ups are judging my management skills; so I'm held accountable for the motivation and quality of the work performed by everyone who works for me.

"There are fifteen people in my department, including support staff," Meg said. "Until recently, Norm was the only problem I had. Now, a lot of other people are getting demoralized and upset by him. Understandably, they hold me responsible since, after all, I'm the manager. So, I'm looking at a potential mutiny of my whole marketing department if I don't find some way to get Norm in line.

"The thing that's so infuriating about him is that he never comes out and says anything directly against me or anyone else. Two weeks ago, I had a meeting with senior management. The marching orders they gave me were to develop and implement three big promotional campaigns for new products that we're introducing. I was expected to report back in a week with a budget, timetable, and detailed plans for the first campaign.

"Since Norm is responsible for special promotional projects, naturally I called him and others in my department to a meeting and laid out the assignment. I thought Norm would be excited about these new projects. Instead, he was very sulky and argumentative at the meeting. Every time someone came up with an idea, he would find some reason to knock it down, claiming that it wouldn't work or that it was too difficult, or some other objection. In any case, I made it very clear to Norm that I needed a draft of the plans, budget, and timetable on my desk within four days.

"So, what does Norm do?" Meg asked rhetorically. "Absolutely nothing. When I confronted him about not doing the assignment, he said that he had thought the deadline was in ten days instead of four; besides, he felt that management was being unreasonable in their demands and that he was doing his best.

"By the next day, he had done the timetable but nothing else. Given the pressure that was on the department, I couldn't believe how slowly he was working. To make a long story short, I wound up working around the clock for two days. Then I was reprimanded by senior management for blowing the deadline. Consequently, I broke out in hives and had tension headaches for days afterward." Meg sighed.

"The pattern is always the same with him. Norm's actually a talented guy. I need him very much—or someone in his position—in order for my department to function effectively. But he always puts things off and blows deadlines; or he forgets about meetings or important assignments. When he says he has too much work to do, I tell him to delegate to his support staff, but he never does.

"Last week," Meg continued, "he came to an important meeting with our outside advertising agency and didn't have the necessary materials in his briefcase. He said that he'd misplaced them and would look for them when he got back to the office. So the meeting turned out to be a total waste of time and I wound up looking and feeling stupid and incompetent.

"Apparently, he behaves this way in other relationships, too—not just because he resents me. I talked with an ex-girlfriend of his who works at the company. They dated for about two years, and the ex-girlfriend was very candid with me in our conversation. According to her experience, Norm hadn't started acting flaky until she started to make a few demands of him—she wanted to see him more often and was looking for a commitment.

"I guess that made him angry. But, according to her, he

never said so. What he did was to start forgetting to do certain favors for her that he had promised; or showing up late for their dates. She said the straw that broke the camel's back was when her parents came to visit her from out of town. She wanted Norm to meet them for dinner but he wasn't too keen on the idea.

"But," Meg described, "instead of just saying that he would rather not have dinner with them, he went along and refused to talk to anyone. He was sullen and withdrawn for the whole evening. His girlfriend about flipped out when they got home. Norm said that he just couldn't understand why she was so upset. He denied having done anything wrong—he pointed out that he hadn't said anything to offend them. When she explained to Norm that not talking at all was incredibly rude, he refused to see her point of view. They broke up a short time later.

"I envy her because she was able to get out of the relationship," Meg said. "I can't—at least not if I want to keep my job. I'm starting to itch again just thinking about how infuriating this guy is."

Meg's description of Norm matches that of a classic passive-aggressive personality disorder. Norm's behavior is, in fact, quite hostile, which is why it elicits so much hostility and frustration from others in response. However, his aggression is couched in a thin veil of passivity—he makes people furious through passive resistance to their demands.

His resistance is expressed indirectly rather than directly. In other words, Norm doesn't assert himself other than to whine and complain about the "unreasonable" demands people make on him. Instead, he "forgets" what is required of him, or he procrastinates, or he exhibits his resistance to a situation by refusing to be socially appropriate, as was the case with his refusal to converse with his ex-girlfriend's parents.

The most common maneuvers used by passive-aggressive

personalities are procrastination, dawdling, stubbornness, intentional inefficiency, and forgetfulness.

Meg's efforts to do a good job in her managerial position were continually foiled by Norm's obstructive behavior. Typical of the disorder, Norm protests to other people about how "unreasonable" Meg and senior management are, and he sulks, becomes irritable, or argues when he is asked to do something that he does not wish to do. But his arguments are not direct. Often, such people are scornful of those in authority positions, though the contempt is expressed behind the backs of the authority figures.

In a word, passive-aggressive personalities are maddening. Their behavior almost invariably elicits hostility from those with whom they interact.

Fatal Personality #4: The Addictive Personality

Technically, the addiction-prone personality does not fall into the psychiatric category of "personality disorders," but few would disagree with the designation of such individuals as "fatal personalities." Spend one evening at an Al-Anon meeting (spouses, children, and other codependents of alcoholics and drug abusers) and you'll get an instant picture of the suffering—both physical and psychological—that addicts cause to those who are involved with them.

There has been a widespread movement afoot in this country over the last decade to broaden the application of the term *addiction*. Whereas it used to apply to individuals who were dependent on alcohol and/or other substances, the concept has more recently come to describe anyone who relates to an activity in an excessive, compulsive, and out-of-control fashion. Thus, we now hear of sex addiction, love addiction, food addiction, gambling addiction, shopping addiction, and other forms of excessive behavior.

Along with the explosive growth of those counted as addicts of one kind or another, and a profitable industry based on treating the myriad addictions, there has been yet another group that has similarly expanded its numbers: the codependents. These are the people who, in effect, are addicted to people who are addicted.

Since addiction, by definition, makes its object (e.g., alcohol, gambling, etc.) the number-one priority, other people in an addict's life necessarily take a backseat. The exception is when the addiction itself is to another person, in which case the partner is obsessively needed in a way that becomes depersonalizing. In other words, if you are needed like a drug, you eventually will be treated and *used* in much the same way.

Addicts notoriously lie, deny, exploit others, and wreak havoc with their families, work, and social relationships. Therefore, wives or husbands of such Lethal Lovers suffer the humiliation, depression, uncertainty, frustration, hostility, debilitation of self-esteem, and other toxic emotions that the addict creates.

The addict's extreme neediness—which becomes greater as the addiction worsens and debilitation increases—fits the excessive, complementary need of the codependent to take care of others at the expense of his or her own health and well-being. Thus, the addict's problems become highly detrimental not only to himself or herself but to the codependent personality with whom he or she is linked.

People who are intimately involved with addicts try nearly everything to get their partners to stop drinking, using drugs, gambling, and so forth. But, until the addict decides to change, nothing anyone else does will make a difference. Indeed, the partner's actions will be futile; nothing he or she tries will get the desired result.

Some years ago, an oncologist asked me to see his patient, Grace, a lovely 62-year-old woman who had terminal and very painful metastasized bone cancer. While Grace had accepted her imminent death, she could find no peace because her husband, Bill, was drowning in an alcoholic bender that had been going on nonstop for nearly a month.

The couple (both previously widowed) had been married for only three years. Grace knew that Bill had had serious problems with alcohol following his first wife's death. But he had been sober for more than a year when they met, and Grace believed that by providing him with a happy life and financial comfort (Grace's first husband had left her with a lot of money), Bill would simply cease needing alcohol. But Grace had married an addictive personality, and, like other partners of alcoholics, she erroneously assumed responsibility for keeping him sober.

Shortly after they arrived home from their honeymoon, Grace and Bill had a serious argument over finances. His response was to get drunk and stay that way for three days. Grace blamed herself for Bill's fall off the wagon because she had gotten angry with him about money. So, she gave in on the point of contention and Bill received the money he wanted.

Thereafter, a destructive pattern was set in motion. Whenever Bill got angry or upset with Grace, he would punish her (and himself) by getting drunk. Grace then would blame herself for his drinking, believing that she had done something "wrong" since, she reasoned, he would otherwise have remained sober. So, Grace swallowed her toxic feelings—her anger, anxiety, and depression—so that she wouldn't set Bill off on a drinking binge.

When Grace was diagnosed with terminal cancer, her first reaction was guilt. All she could think of was how much Bill would suffer when he learned of her illness and of how she had "let him down."

"He loved his first wife so much and when she died it nearly killed him," Grace told me. "Now look at what I'm doing—the very same thing. I feel so guilty."

Grace had grown up in an alcoholic home and therefore had all the requisite conditions for becoming a codependent personality. Whenever her father got drunk, her mother said that Grace was responsible because she had done something to upset him. Understandably, then, Grace's psyche was conditioned to take responsibility for Bill's addiction.

171

Of course, nobody could say precisely what caused Grace's cancer. But her oncologist and I agreed that Grace's style of emotional suppression combined with Bill's alcoholism certainly created a lethal environment.

The most poignant memory I have of Bill and Grace was a conversation that took place at their home only a few days before her death. Bill had stopped drinking for about a week, but his sobriety was wobbly at best; and Grace's pain, even with medication, was apparent. We talked about their relationship and they both acknowledged their love and dependency on each other. Then, in a moment of rare clarity and candor, each talked about how responsible they felt for the problems that had befallen the other.

Predictably, though, after Grace died, Bill stayed drunk for almost six months. And during that period, he went through a substantial portion of the money Grace had left him.

The Big Hook: Trying to Change a Fatal Personality

People in my PMMS workshops speak of other types of "fatal personalities," but the four I've described remain the most difficult and, arguably, the most damaging. The common thread that links PMMS participants is their futile efforts to change the difficult, damaging people in their lives.

Personality disorders and addictive personalities are defined in part by the disruption they cause to interpersonal relationships. So, the defining features of individuals with personality disorders are sufficient to produce psychological poisons in others with whom they are involved.

For many members of the PMMS workshops—and others like them—those toxic emotions are compounded by their compulsive drive to fix the disordered personalities of their Lethal Lovers or other poisonous people in their lives. The hook that keeps many of them enmeshed in relationships so injurious to their emotional and physical health is their egos.

One man in the PMMS group put it this way: "I'm not a stupid or careless guy. I was married once before and I must have dated hundreds of women in the ten years that I waited to remarry. I thought I knew what I was doing and that I was sophisticated and cautious enough to make a good selection.

"It took me six years to realize I was married to a woman with a borderline personality disorder," he explained. "I didn't want to see it; my ego wouldn't allow it. Acknowledging that she was so screwed up meant I also had to acknowledge that I had made a huge, whopping error in judgment. I had been taken in by her manipulations and I hated myself for being so damn stupid and weak.

"Then," he continued, "it took me another three years to get divorced because I kept thinking there was something I could do to make her different. In therapy, I finally realized that my real issue wasn't about her; it was about me. In other words, I couldn't come to terms with *my* mistake; I needed to make her better so I wouldn't look bad in my own eyes.

"Eventually, the stress of the relationship got so bad that it had become a matter of my physical survival," he concluded. "I was becoming seriously ill, and the reason had a lot to do with how angry I was with her and with myself. When I finally forgave myself and admitted that I'd made a mistake, that I'd misjudged her, and that I couldn't fix her, I gave myself permission to leave. And I've been a whole lot healthier and happier since."

Personality disorders are exceedingly difficult to change even when the patient is motivated and the therapist is highly skilled. People involved with fatal personalities, whose own egos drive them to fix or change their disturbed partners, merely set themselves up to fail.

So, trying to change a Lethal Lover or fatal personality is *not* the way out of the dilemma. But there are methods for detoxifying some poisonous relationships and for saving yourself from the damaging effects of others.

Those methods are what we turn to now in Part Two: The Solution.

PART TWO

The
Solution

14

A User's Guide to Part Two

Dr. Hans Selye's solution to the problem of Lethal Lovers and toxic relationships is this: Cut the person (or people) causing you stress out of your life.[22]

Appealing as such a solution is in its presumed simplicity and directness, the fact is that few of us can merely "cut" people out of our lives altogether—certainly not without considerable anguish and inner turmoil; nor, in many cases, would we even want to. There are, for example, family blood ties that may be the cause of a great deal of stress but that nevertheless form part of the fabric of our lives. Employment relationships may be exceedingly stressful, but economic circumstances and situational pressures may preclude any quick solution that involves simply walking away from the job.

On the other hand, Dr. Selye does offer sound and sage advice, however overstated or oversimplified his solution may appear. The stress of toxic relationships can be immense, even life threatening. If the choice comes down to staying in a relationship that could well be killing you, versus finding a way to cut yourself loose, then the choice of your survival should prevail.

One of the greatest pressures toxic relationships produce is prolonged *decisional stress*—the back-and-forth confusion over whether to stay with the relationship (trying to change it somehow for the better or merely endure the pain and problems) or leave the relationship, thereby facing the unknown pain ahead that such a choice might yield. This is the proverbial choice between the devil you know versus the devil you don't know.

I cannot offer you a simple guide to these turning points in life since they depend on highly individualized circumstances, values, personalities, and specific issues. However, I can provide you with a framework for understanding how harmful relationships can be detoxified. A great deal of decisional stress arises from not even knowing how to begin the process of fixing a damaged relationship.

First, therefore, I will identify what the positive, health-promoting qualities of relationships are and what you can do to build those qualities into your existing relationships, thereby *diluting* or *removing* the toxins as much as possible. I hope also to sensitize you to the *ongoing* need to nurture and maintain the presence of positive emotions in your relationship as a process to which you and your partner must remain permanently committed.

But I also must tell you that not all relationships can or should be saved. In some cases, the toxic emotions become so overwhelmingly prevalent that any positive feelings are destroyed.

Moreover, the continuation of an irreversibly toxic relationship and the health of one or both of the partners could be mutually exclusive. In other words, if the relationship continues, one or both members must sacrifice their physical and emotional health. Conversely, if the good health of the individuals is to be preserved or rebuilt, the relationship must terminate. In such cases, the goal of preserving the relationship serves no one.

If you have identified yourself as a partner to a Lethal Lover (or *as* a Lethal Lover), or if you see yourself as a participant in another type of toxic relationship, you face some difficult choices. Your first decision must be whether to commit yourself to the effort of trying to preserve the relationship by changing the balance of negative and positive emotions.

The remainder of this book is intended to serve a twofold purpose. First, by reading what is entailed in the process of detoxifying harmful relationships and maintaining healthy ones, you will be in a far better position to make that critical first decision. Keep in mind that love relationships require the cooperation and commitment of both partners in order for effective changes to occur. In others, such as employment or family relationships, the change may have to be all one-sided—*your* side. Therefore, you must determine the extent to which you can unilaterally alter the way you react, given that the other person's behavior does not change.

The second intended purpose is to provide you with a *guide to behavior*. If, after reading through this section, you decide to work on changing your current relationship, the book will direct your actions in very concrete, specific ways.

Alternatively, if your decision directs you out of your current relationship, the behavioral guide will help you set out to *create* a new, healthier relationship in its place.

Keep in mind that rebuilding a healthy relationship is an ongoing *process*. You must approach the solution to your relationship problems as a continuum rather than a black-or-white, all-or-nothing, quick-change event. This implies the need for commitment, patience, and endurance. It also requires that you learn to evaluate your relationship in relative terms: Relative to the way it was, is it getting better? Relative to the way it is now, how can it further improve? Let's find out.

15

❧══════❧══════❧

Antidotes to Psychological Poisons

People who have been exposed to the prolonged stress of a toxic relationship cannot think straight.

This is because intense stress compromises cognitive reasoning and leaves its victims feeling confused, overwhelmed, out of control, and directionless with respect to how to cope with their plight. As we examined earlier, loss of control, helplessness, and inability to cope are the psychological poisons most toxic to physical health.

So, if you are involved with a Lethal Lover or are in another kind of toxic relationship, the first thing I want to do is help you regain your all-important *sense of control*. This is an immediate antidote to psychological poisoning and will help quell the feelings of panic, anxiety, and depression that intensify your negative emotions. Remember, the *perception* that you are out of control of your stressors is strongly correlated with compromised immune function; the *sense* that you *are* in control is protective of immune function.

Focusing and Organizing Your Thoughts About Relationships

When you feel overwhelmed by emotions—particularly negative ones—it becomes quite difficult to conceive of a rational, objective way to think about relationships. And if you can't think logically about what a relationship is or should be, you can't possibly know how to make yours better.

For now, then, let me do the thinking for you. Your job is simply to read the ideas that follow and use them as pegs on which to organize your jumbled thoughts. As your thinking begins to clear, your sense of control will increase.

Your Relationship Investment

Think of a relationship as an investment. There are many things that you invest, depending on the type of relationship. For purposes of clarity, I will focus on love relationships, with the understanding that the basic principles apply to any type of bond. Time, effort, money, love, self-esteem, material objects, sexuality, affection, hopes, dreams—and whatever other assets you wish to add—constitute the psychological and material investment you put into your intimate relationships.

Just as every investment involves costs as well as rewards, so does every relationship. Think of the psychological rewards as the positive, good feelings you derive as a result of being in the relationship; the costs, in turn, are the negative, toxic feelings that the relationship creates. Of course, there are also material rewards and costs, but we are most concerned here with the psychological dimension of your investment.

What makes an investment *profitable* is a positive ratio of rewards to costs. In simple terms, a good investment is one in which the rewards you receive exceed the costs you incur; that is what generates the profit. Conversely, a bad investment is one in which the incurred costs exceed the derived rewards; that is what makes it a losing proposition.

When a relationship becomes toxic, the costs drastically overrun the rewards. In order to turn your relationship around toward the path of profitability, you will need to find ways to boost the rewards you get from it while, at the same time, developing ways to reduce the costs.

Keep in mind this key concept of *ratio* of rewards to costs as the basis of overall profit. Even if your costs are relatively high in a relationship, you may still find it to be a good investment if your rewards are far higher. Of course, this is subjective.

This model suggests that in order to "fix" your relationship, you don't necessarily have to begin by figuring out how to solve all your problems. In fact, as you now know from having focused on your negative feelings for so long, that approach is probably what has demoralized you and, frankly, confused your thinking.

A smarter way to begin, then, is to focus on the emotional, psychological rewards that your relationship currently provides, used to provide, or might provide in the future. You will need strategies, of course, for boosting the number and frequency of those emotional payoffs from your investment.

Before you move on to learning those strategies, you first need to better understand the nature of rewards in relationships and the qualities of relationships that allow people to derive their profits.

The Power of Positive Emotions

The biggest payoffs you can derive from any relationship are the opportunities to experience the positive emotions of life. Many recent best-selling authors have written compellingly of the influence of positive emotions on the body's ability to ward off illness and promote healing.

Happily, the full range of positive emotions is far too long to enumerate. However, there is a general consensus among these leading experts that the most important are: love, optimism, hope, sense of purpose, will to live, faith, pleasure, determination, festivity and laughter, peacefulness, high self-esteem, altruism, and a sense of support from others. These positive emotions have been demonstrated to heighten immune strength, enhance resistance to illness, alter dangerous cardiovascular trends, and otherwise to save or prolong lives.

Certainly, no responsible psychologist, psychoneuroimmunology researcher, or any other proponent of utilizing positive emotions to activate the body's natural healing mechanisms recommends doing so to the exclusion of traditional medical care. On the contrary, such emotions are to be used as critically important adjuncts to the best available medical treatment. However, by detoxifying your negative relationships, creating positive ones, and terminating those lethal ties that are not reversible (or not worth reversing), you can go a long way toward saving, prolonging, and enhancing your life.

Creating a Positive Emotional Climate

The first step in your overall strategy is to learn to create the best emotional environment for your relationship in order to maximize the rewards. You may wish, for example, to feel more love and emotional support from your partner. But if the two of you don't sit down together to communicate your feelings, needs, and fears, the *context* will not exist for you to experience what you desire.

Positive emotions are as delicate and precious as rare orchids. In order for the flowers to bloom and flourish, the best possible climatic conditions, soil, and light are necessary. Positive emotions, too, will flourish only if an optimal emotional climate is created and maintained.

In love relationships, positive emotions blossom when both partners determine to be as open and communicative with each other as they are capable of being. This is the requisite condition for feelings of all kinds—but especially for positive ones—to come forth.

Next, positive emotions, like orchids, do not do well in cold climates. They require a warm, sometimes even steamy, environment. Warmth can be created and expressed through touching, physical affection, smiling, acts of kindness, pats on the back, and sexual intimacy.

Next, an overall attitude of mutual respect is mandatory for healthy emotions to develop in relationships. Respect is shown in numerous ways—through what you do and say as well as what you do not do or say. For example, mutual respect is demonstrated by listening and valuing each other's conversation; by taking pride in the accomplishments of each other and of yourselves as a couple; and by using language with reference to the other that connotes esteem.

Respect is shown also by *not* using derogatory, patronizing, or otherwise demeaning language toward each other either when alone or with others; by *not* ignoring or dismissing each other's opinions or ideas; and by *not* negating or invalidating each other's feelings or reactions.

Positive emotions thrive only when the environment is emotionally safe. They cannot take root when the climate is fraught with fear, anxiety, unpredictability, or dishonesty. A safe environment is created by partners trying to the best of their abilities to honor each other with honesty; to fulfill agreements, vows, contracts, and promises; and to behave with reasonable consistency and predictability. That is how mutual trust is reaffirmed.

Many of the healing emotions such as faith, optimism, purpose, determination, hope, and will to live derive in part from an explicit, shared statement of values within the relationship. Partners who mutually define the purpose and meaning of their special relationship create something together in which they can believe and have faith. Behavior that is faithful to the values of the partnership furthers its purposes and strengthens the foundation from which both members can meet future uncertainties.

Finally, the optimal climate for positive emotions is one that is fun and pleasurable. Playfulness, laughter, spontaneity, and humor are healing emotions. They also foster the development and growth of further positive feelings. Physical and psychological pleasure are strong antidotes to depression, anxiety, stress, and other toxic emotions.

Developing an Overlapping Life Space

When a relationship is flooded with toxic emotions, partners frequently react by seeking refuge in activities or people outside of it. As a consequence, the identity of the relationship—as something more than or different from merely the sum of two individuals—becomes obscured or even lost.

To fully appreciate the importance of this point, you must understand that there are *three* components to a love relationship: you, your partner, and the relationship itself. This third dimension—the "us"—represents the *identity* of the relationship.

When partners distance themselves from each other by avoiding shared time, conversation, and joint activities, the net result is that there is no "us" there.

A relationship's mode of interaction must be identifiable in order for it to be the object of any kind of remedy. Moreover, there must be a clear sense of "us" so that the partners can feel more positive toward each other and toward the relationship itself. It is at least as important—if not more so—to be in love with your relationship as it is with your partner.

The most direct way to create or recreate the "us" is to find more ways to overlap each other's life space. Every individual has areas of activity or engagement in life—called his or her "life space"—which might include work, leisure activities, social involvements, child rearing, family obligations, community participation, and so forth. By finding ways to intersect these areas of your respective lives, the sense of "us" will emerge.

This means that a basic commitment of time spent together, preferably in several different areas of your respective life spaces, is mandatory for the "us" identity to solidify and for your relationship to become detoxified. How much time is the right amount? That's a matter of individual preference and a subject for negotiation between you and your partner.

Clearly, of course, the amount of time you will want to spend together is a function of how rewarding your relationship is. If your time together is miserable, neither of you will want to invest much more of it in the relationship. But, as you increase positive emotions and reduce toxic ones, the "us" will become far more valuable, and the time and effort required to preserve and protect it will be well worthwhile.

Do the Behavior First, Your Mind Will Follow

If you are involved in a toxic relationship, your first reaction to the notion of developing a positive emotional climate and overlapping life spaces probably will be resistance. You won't *want* to do any of the things described above or in the chapters that follow because you now feel too angry, depressed, burned out, pessimistic, or stubborn to believe that anything will make much difference in your damaged relationship. Of course, this is the core mindset of learned helplessness.

Do not assume that you must first *feel* positive emotions before you can change your behavior. If that were a valid precondition, few toxic relationships would stand a chance of cure since the partners, by definition, often no longer have many positive feelings. In fact, what initially motivates people to rescue a poisoned relationship is not so much that they *want* to stay because of the positive feelings they have, but rather that they do *not* want to leave. In other words, they wish to avoid further, and potentially worse, negative feelings.

The more effective course is simply to *do the behavior* designed to create positive feelings, regardless of the fact that your mind or heart may not be similarly inclined. Counterintuitive though it seems, behavior change is frequently the *cause* of alterations in moods, feelings, and attitudes, rather than the result.

If you have committed yourself to a course of trying to detoxify a negative relationship, then acting in ways that may not yet be entirely consistent with your feelings is neither hypocritical nor false. On the contrary, by trying to behave in a manner that is more affectionate or considerate, even though your actions may be somewhat forced, you are following a proven strategy for generating positive emotions.

186

The Antidote Mindset

There is a critically important role that your mind must play if you are to reach the desired goal of curing your toxic relationship. Although your feelings toward the relationship and your partner are not yet sufficiently positive, your overall mindset toward the detoxification process must be.

To best counteract psychological poisons, your mental approach should embrace the three essential elements of *control*, *challenge*, and *commitment*, which I discussed in chapter 2. These, you will recall, constitute the secret of psychological hardiness—the attitudes that allow certain individuals to handle high amounts of stress without succumbing to its negative effects and, indeed, often to benefit from it.

First, concentrate on the fact that by developing a constructive way to think about your relationship and practicing the techniques described in the pages that follow, you will be breaking out of a purely reactive cycle and into a healthier, more proactive mode. You will be initiating new behaviors instead of merely doing the dangerous dance you and your partner have so long rehearsed. In so doing, you will be exercising *control*.

Second, accept that change inevitably involves stress. However, you are now prepared to welcome the *challenge* of accomplishing your goals with an attitude of hopeful anticipation and confidence.

Finally, keep foremost in your mind the *commitment* you have made to getting healthier. Your efforts to detoxify your relationship are meant to improve the quality of your emotional life as well as your physical well-being. In this context, working to make your relationship more positive takes on a greater, deeper meaning in that it serves to both prolong and enhance the process of life itself.

16

How to Detoxify Your Relationship

I. Techniques for Diluting Toxic Emotions

Think of your toxic relationship as a patient who has swallowed poison. The toxins that threaten the survival of the relationship are the negative emotions—helplessness, depression, cynicism, hostility, anxiety, loss of self-esteem, frustration, and hopelessness—felt by you, and perhaps by your partner. The time now has come to commence the patient's detoxification.

Following the medical metaphor, you will use three treatment strategies. In this chapter, you will learn techniques to *dilute* the poisons by flushing your relationship's system with positive emotions. In this way, the harmful concentration of toxic feelings will be thinned out and weakened.

In subsequent chapters, you will learn to *purge* relationship toxins and to *neutralize* them with proper antidotes.

Your relationship's prognosis depends, to a large extent, on the degree to which both you and your partner are committed to its recovery and survival. In particular, the detoxification of love relationships requires that both partners work together toward creating a healthier bond.

However, some degree of change can be accomplished even when the effort is made only unilaterally. In such cases, the modification of one partner's behavior can be sufficient to induce alterations—conscious or otherwise—in the actions and feelings of the other. Unilateral change may indeed be the only option in certain instances, such as employment relationships, nonvoluntary family ties, or with an intractable partner when other factors (such as children) weigh against leaving. In such cases, protecting *your* health may necessitate working solely on your side of the problem, since the other person will not cooperate.

The majority of techniques that follow are described for use by partners in a love relationship, and most assume the cooperative efforts of both. However, the basic principles of each method are applicable to almost all toxic relationships. So, with appropriate adaptation, you can use the techniques to detoxify other harmful bonds in your life.

Be sure to give the patient—your toxic relationship—adequate opportunity to respond to the treatment. It undoubtedly took time for the toxins to build up, and it will necessarily take further time for the patient to rally back to health.

How Long Will the Process Take to Work?

Since every relationship is different, absolute time prescriptions are impossible. There is, however, an axiom that a psychological crisis lasts for about six weeks. By definition, a crisis is a turning point for better or worse. In this sense, your relationship now has reached a crisis of toxicity, and the process of detoxification that you are about to begin represents the turning point.

My recommendation is that you try to suspend judgment of whether the process is working for a period of at least six weeks. Put aside your considerations of the outcome and focus all your energy instead on the task of getting the patient—your relationship—through the crisis.

After six weeks of conscientiously practicing the following techniques, you should have a fairly clear idea of whether your relationship has turned the corner and is headed toward recovery; or whether, instead, it has either failed to improve or, worse, has deteriorated further.

If the outcome is hopeful after six weeks, the momentum of positive change will propel you forward with continued, redoubled efforts to make your relationship's recovery complete. Remember: The process of improvement is never-ending.

On the other hand, should no appreciable change for the better occur after six weeks, it will be necessary for you to reevaluate your options. If you have not already sought professional help, now is the time to do so. You may be able to acknowledge ways in which you failed to give your best effort to the techniques. If this is the case, it makes good sense to extend the process for another six weeks, provided you can summon the necessary motivation to give your best effort. After three months, you should know whether your relationship is responding positively to the detoxification process.

As I cautioned previously, some relationships are so highly toxic that they cannot—and should not—be saved. In these cases, the poisonous emotions have wreaked such severe damage on the partners that the detoxification process simply will not be effective. Nor will the most skilled therapist be able, or indeed willing, to preserve the bond at the expense of the health of the individuals involved.

Techniques for Diluting Toxic Relationships with Positive Emotions

Toxic relationships, by definition, are characterized by high concentrations of negative feelings. This means that the way the partners behave—or fail to behave—toward each other generates intense negative emotions on a frequent and regular basis.

In addition, toxic relationships are characterized by a higher ratio of negative to positive feelings, causing a demoralizing and destabilizing factor in the relationship. The detoxification process requires that the concentration of toxins be diluted through an infusion of positive feelings. Only then will the balance shift and the motivation to preserve and improve the relationship be regained.

Following are ten techniques for diluting toxins by generating positive emotions that I have used very successfully with my patients over the years.

1. Inventory of rewards. To begin, take a careful inventory of the good things that exist in your relationship. You and your partner should develop the reward inventories independently. Ask yourself these questions:

- What are the psychological payoffs or positive feelings for me *now* in this relationship?
- What are the good things or benefits that I receive *now* from this relationship and/or from my partner?

Write your answers in the form of a list; title your list "Current Rewards." Force yourself to identify as many positive aspects of your relationship as you can—both psychological (e.g., feelings of love and security) and concrete or external (e.g., good sex; money to spend on luxuries).

Next, ask yourself the same questions in the past tense:

- What *were* the psychological payoffs or positive feelings that I used to get from the relationship?
- What *were* the good things or benefits that I *used* to receive from my relationship and/or from my partner?

Title your second list "Past Rewards."

Finally, make a third list, called "Future Rewards." This should include some of the past rewards that you would like to regain, as well as payoffs or benefits that you have never realized but would most like to receive from your relationship and/or partner in the future.

Make each list as thorough as possible. When you have completed your inventory, review your lists and circle the three most valuable rewards on each.

Next, compare your lists with your partner's. This will enable you to better understand your partner's needs and values and give you a snapshot perspective of how much agreement or similarity exists between you. Pay particular attention to those items that are common to both inventories.

The inventory will help to make the positive features of your relationship—either past or present—more salient in your mind. The current level of toxicity probably has distorted your thinking toward the negative, so that whatever good does or might again exist in the relationship has become largely obscured.

Discuss the lists with your partner as thoroughly as you can. Share the insights and new understandings the exercise has given you about yourself and your partner. Talking together about the positive feelings that you currently have, used to have, and hold as goals for the future will increase your sense of "us" and cast a more favorable light on your relationship.

2. Fulfilling needs. Having your emotional needs met is one of the most important payoffs your relationship can provide. This exercise will teach you to ask your partner directly to help meet those needs. It also will encourage you to listen and respond to your partner's requests.

Begin by writing down a description, in general terms, of a need you would like fulfilled by your partner within the next three days. Examples might include, "I need to feel loved," "I have sexual needs that I want fulfilled," or, "I need to feel better about myself." The stated need may be anything you want as long as it is something that your partner can fulfill or help you to fulfill. Your partner will write down his or her need at the same time.

Next, take your generally stated need and formulate a behavioral method in which your partner can help fulfill your need. For example, if your stated need is to feel more loved, you might ask your partner to tell you his or her positive feelings about you, or to show affection through hugging and kissing, or to do you a special favor.

The key to this technique is to identify very clearly *how* your partner can act to meet your need. Too often, needs are left either unstated or stated so generally that your partner remains at a loss to know just what to do in order to fulfill your requests.

Focus on keeping your request positive and clear. Don't explain your need by criticizing what your partner has failed to do in the past. Simply ask him or her to help fulfill your need now. And take turns.

Then, tell your partner *exactly* what you would like him or her *to do* in order to meet your need.

When both of you have made your requests and provided your behavioral prescriptions, set a time limit of three days for fulfillment of your promises. Make an agreement to meet with each other on the fourth day to discuss the results of the exercise. Use that opportunity to provide feedback to each other about how it felt to have your partner try to respond to your stated need.

Repeat the exercise twice more or until asking for what you need becomes second nature.

3. Unselfish acts as a show of love. One of the clearest ways to demonstrate your love is to do something for your partner that is unselfish, altruistic, or not in your self-interest. The act need not be a grand gesture. On the contrary, small actions, performed consistently and done for your partner's benefit instead of yours, will add up to a strong, ongoing expression of love.

Make an agreement with your partner that every day for one week, you each will do something strictly for the other's benefit. For example, you might do your partner a favor, or buy a present, run an errand, eat at his or her favorite restaurant, engage in an activity together that is more pleasurable to your partner than to you, and so forth. The important thing is that you each try to do something that is clearly in your partner's self-interest rather than in your own.

Over the course of the week, sensitize yourself to your partner's actions. Make a note of all the things your partner does that show positive feelings toward you. Be sure to acknowledge your partner's actions and show your appreciation. At week's end, talk about the exercise and discuss the differences in the way you feel about each other as a result of the exercise.

4. Building self-esteem by giving and receiving positive feedback. When a relationship turns toxic, communication is often restricted to a negative-feedback cycle. This means that you both may be mired in giving and receiving criticism, or expressing anger, demands, bitterness, and even insults. Or perhaps you are simply ignoring each other. This technique is designed to break the negative-feedback cycle and to replace it with positivity.

Find a place where you and your partner can be alone together with little or no distractions. Your purpose is to spend ten to fifteen minutes providing each other with honest, positive feedback.

You may use any of the following, or a combination, to help structure your exchange:

- Take a few minutes to thoroughly observe each other's physical appearance. Openly state at least three things that you like about the way your partner looks.
- Say what you consider your partner's three greatest personality or character strengths; provide clear behavioral examples to illustrate each.
- Tell at least one positive way in which your partner is special or distinct from most other people you know; give examples; explain why you value this in your partner.

- State at least two things that you think your partner does particularly well; give clear examples.
- Tell your partner in what way(s) you would like to be more like him or her; give examples; say why you value this trait in your partner.

5. Delighting your partner. Make an agreement with your partner that you will each try to do something for the other designed to produce feelings of surprise, delight, or amusement. Leave the time frame ambiguous—e.g., "sometime within the next month." The "delight" you plan may coincide with a special occasion such as a birthday or holiday. Or you may want to spontaneously enchant your partner for no reason other than the pure pleasure of doing so.

Putting creative energy into this exercise will help to reawaken the childlike qualities within you that are essential to the healing experiences of festivity, laughter, and pleasure as adults. Planning something delightful, and anticipating your partner's response, helps evoke a more generally positive orientation toward the future, from which the healing emotions of hope, optimism, and faith derive.

6. Getting and giving emotional support. The ability to approach your partner for emotional support and to receive it are among the most valuable payoffs from a close relationship. Of course, the reciprocal experiences of feeling needed by your partner for support and of being capable of responding are equally rewarding.

First, you and your partner each must identify a future situation that you anticipate might be stressful, difficult, or uncomfortable and for which, therefore, you desire emotional support. For example, you are scheduled for a performance review with your boss or you plan to discuss a touchy situation with a friend or parent.

Tell your partner about the situation and specifically about the aspects over which you have concern. Your partner should take care to listen to and accept your feelings and should resist challenging your reaction or jumping to premature advice giving. Emotional support, in the first place, involves being a good, *noncritical* listener.

Next, describe how you want to handle the situation. If you desire, ask your partner for an opinion, advice, or observations. However, your partner should not initiate such commentary, as it might be misinterpreted as criticism. If you are clear about how to handle the anticipated situation, you may need or want your partner only to bolster your decisions.

Try to be as clear as possible about the kind of emotional support you need. For example, you might ask your partner to role-play the situation with you, or to telephone you before and after the event, or just to provide reassuring words of encouragement.

When your partner speaks of the need for emotional support from you, follow the same instructions. Be sure you ask whatever questions are necessary to fully understand the particular ways in which your partner wants you to demonstrate support for him or her.

This technique provides effective emotional support in the face of an anticipated stress and trains partners in how to be effective support givers. Repeated practice of this technique also will enhance your mutual sense of being needed emotionally by the other.

7. Showing positive emotions nonverbally. Sometimes, a gentle touch, warm embrace, pat on the back, or passionate kiss is worth far more than mere words. Infusing your relationship with positive emotions is best done through both verbal *and* nonverbal means of expression.

Begin by agreeing with your partner to select, at random, a "nonverbal expression day" for each of you. To do this, simply write out the names of the days of the week on seven slips of paper. Fold the slips and put them in a paper bag. Then, you and your partner draw one slip each to determine your respective days for nonverbal expression in the coming week. Do not tell each other the outcome of the draw.

196

When the day you have drawn arrives, your task is to express *nonverbally* as many positive emotions toward your partner as you can. The range of emotions might include appreciation (shaking hands), affection (hugs), lust (a passionate kiss), love, reassurance (a pat on the back), amusement, and a host of others.

The point of the exercise is to sensitize you to the number of ways that nonverbal modes of communication can be used to both express and receive "silent" positive emotions. By constraining yourself for a day to purely nonverbal positive expressions, you will enhance your overall ability to communicate positively.

The side benefit of this exercise is that it is both challenging and fun. It also provides an exaggerated, intentional, and amusing way to break the ice in toxic relationships that have grown unhealthfully distant and cold.

Repeat this exercise often to encourage more frequent occasions of nonverbal expressions.

8. Gearing up for a shared future. Hope, optimism, faith, sense of purpose, and will to live all depend on being oriented positively toward the future. The anxiety inherent in facing the unknown will be greatly ameliorated when you can draw strength from the company of your partner. Moreover, your relationship's identity and meaning derive from your joint vision of the future and from the identification of shared goals.

Once again, you and your partner need first to develop independent lists of desired individual and joint relationship goals for each of the following intervals: the next six months; one year, two years, five years, and ten years from the present. Be as specific as possible in your descriptions. For example, independent goals might be a job promotion, weight loss, or educational attainment. Joint goals might be to enlarge your circle of friends, to purchase a house, or to increase the frequency of lovemaking.

Within each time interval, circle one goal from both your personal and your relationship list that is most important to you. Then, reveal your goals to each other and discuss your assessments of their possible attainment and importance.

Focus specifically on the individual goal for the next six months that you circled as most important. Devise ways to help each other reach your respective personal goals; ask your partner for assistance, always trying to be as specific as possible in your requests.

Then, compare your respective lists of six-month *relationship* goals. By discovering how your goals overlap—or fail to converge—you will increase your insight and understanding of each other. Select a relationship goal together that you both value, and devise a strategy for maximizing the likelihood that your goal will be realized.

9. The talking-time ritual. An important bridge between nonoverlapping life spaces is conversation. Telling each other about your experiences during the periods you spend apart is an essential ongoing activity in a healthy relationship. Therefore, this exercise helps you to develop a ritualized period of time each day that is devoted to conversation.

You and your partner must agree on a specific time of day during which you can spend uninterrupted time alone together just talking. Notwithstanding any scheduling difficulties, you *must* find a time each day just to talk to each other. *No excuses.*

During the first week, you must spend a minimum of ten minutes a day engaged in conversation. You may discuss any subject, provided you respect one caveat: You must each *listen* to the other without interruption.

The more you can disclose to each other about your private thoughts, feelings, or behavior, the more intimate your relationship will become. In psychological terms, intimacy is defined by the degree of self-disclosure in a relationship, rather than by sexual or physical actions. However, if you do not feel able to disclose intimacies, you may stick to other subjects such as politics, the news, amusing anecdotes, or just idle gossip.

After the first week, your talking time should be increased by five minutes. During week two, you will spend fifteen minutes each day in uninterrupted conversation. Remember to observe the rule of respectful listening.

You are to increase the length of your talking time by five minutes each week, until you reach thirty minutes per day in the fifth week. Thereafter, you are to maintain your now established ritual of spending a minimum of thirty minutes a day, alone together, just talking. Naturally, you may spend more time.

At first, the talking time may seem forced or terribly inconvenient, but stick with it. You may, of course, vary the time of your ritual to conform to your schedules—perhaps in the evenings during the week, and during the day on weekends. The important thing is that you commit yourselves to spending this time together. Avoid answering the phone or letting children disturb you. Kids will learn to observe and respect your rituals if they know that you do.

Try to make the contexts and locations of your conversations relaxed and pleasant. Eventually, as your relationship improves, you will look forward to your talking time and to the opportunity to share experiences with your partner.

10. Creating "my days," "your days," and "our days." Some positive emotions, such as peacefulness, sense of purpose, and high self-esteem derive from time spent alone as well as together. The goal of this exercise is to help establish a balance between time alone and time together, with an emphasis on pleasure and relaxation.

At the beginning of every month, you and your partner should sit down with a calendar and select three days: one day for each of you separately that is your special time to spend exactly as you desire; and one day that is allocated as a special day together.

On "my day," your goal should be to spend your time engaged in activities, projects, or leisure pursuits that will increase your relaxation, sense of peacefulness, sense of purpose, determination, or self-esteem. You may, for example, elect to take a class, spend time on a hobby, read, see your friends or family, do volunteer work for a charity or other worthwhile cause, take a drive or walk, or indulge yourself in a beauty make-over from top to bottom. What you do doesn't matter; doing it does.

Your partner's role on these special days for you is to provide whatever support or assistance is necessary in order to make it possible for you to do what you want, such as watching the kids, running errands, coming up with ideas, paying for your activity, or just encouraging you to take advantage of your special day.

The responsibility for planning "our day" should be alternated monthly. The goal of "our day" should be to provide pleasure, fun, relaxation, and the opportunity to have some new experiences together. It is important to be a good sport and be willing to try to enjoy whatever is planned, while withholding criticism. Positive feedback should be given to the planner as much as is possible.

"Our day" may be created as a surprise or collaboratively, although the planner should retain primary decision and preparation responsibility. The concept may be expanded, of course, to "our weekend"—perhaps for special occasions—or longer if you desire.

17

How to Detoxify Your Relationship

II. Techniques for Purging Toxic Emotions

The second method of detoxification seeks to purge emotional poisons from your relationship. To accomplish this, you will use techniques that target and isolate specific problems or sources of stress so that they can be eliminated. You will also learn to extinguish toxic emotions by substituting different, healthier feelings in their place.

Clearly, negative emotions are the most salient feature of toxic relationships. Since it is not possible to rid any relationship entirely of bad feelings, your purpose is to reduce the frequency and intensity of the negativity that currently exists.

As with the techniques in the preceding chapter, the methods that follow are most effective when done by both partners. With slight modification, though, many can be done by only one member of the relationship, with the expectation that even unilateral change can interrupt negative patterns and produce reciprocal change in the partner.

1. Inventory of relationship costs. You and your partner should conduct separate inventories of the seven major problems or deficiencies in your relationship. You are limited to seven because mounting a more lengthy list of problems will likely sabotage your morale and motivation. And, if you can successfully eliminate or reduce the severity of seven major problems, you will be well on your way to detoxifying your relationship.

Next to each of the identified problems, indicate what you think are the main causes or stressors responsible for it. For example, you might identify sexual dissatisfaction or difficulties as one of the relationship's major problems. Your analysis of the cause might be that there is too much anger between you, or perhaps that one of you is too stressed or anxious because of problems at work.

Third, make a list of up to five things that your partner does (or fails to do) that cause you to have negative feelings. Be as specific as possible.

Finally, list up to five things that *you* do (or fail to do) that you believe cause your partner to have negative feelings.

After you each have completed your inventories, sit down together and discuss them. This exercise will help illuminate your respective perceptions of the relationship. It is often the case that two partners have very different views of the same relationship. So, examining, comparing, and discussing your inventories will increase your understanding of each other. To the extent that there is at least some agreement on the main problems, you will have a better sense of where to begin to target your efforts.

Discussing the five things your partner does and five things you do that are contributing to the negativity also will facilitate greater understanding and better communication. It is vital, however, that you resist the knee-jerk reaction of becoming defensive or angry. Since the goal of these techniques is to reduce or eliminate negative feelings, avoid using this exercise or others as opportunities to resume hostilities.

2. Joint problem solving. By the time your relationship has deteriorated to the point of toxicity, your ability to function effectively as collaborative problem solvers has probably been greatly compromised. In fact, you may well have always lacked this ability, which accounts, in part, for why your problems have escalated and remained unresolved.

The method you will use in this exercise is called the Seven Step Solution. By following the procedure, you will learn the *process* of effective problem solving as a couple. Once you have mastered the process, you will find that *any* problem that you confront—as an individual or as a couple—can be tackled successfully with the Seven Step Solution.

The seven essential steps are:

1. *Identify* the problem
2. *Analyze* its causes
3. *Brainstorm* all possible alternative solutions
4. *Evaluate* the pros and cons of each alternative
5. *Select* one solution
6. *Implement* the solution
7. *Evaluate* how the solution works and *reevaluate* the problem

In order to apply the seven steps, go back and independently review the inventory of your relationship's major problems. Decide which of the problems you have listed is the *least* serious.

Next, openly discuss the problem together to *arrive at an understanding of how your partner views the cause of the problem* and *for your partner to understand clearly your perception of its cause.*

Remember that the overall purpose of the exercise is to practice problem solving, *not* to trigger an argument. Consequently, be careful not to become defensive, start an argument, or rise to your partner's bait. You must analyze the causes of the problem as objectively as possible.

Step Three is perhaps the most important since under conditions of stress certain cognitive changes take place. Among those changes is something called *cognitive constriction* or *premature closure*. This means that under stress, your mind cannot and does not take into account the full range of possible solutions to any given problem.

To a great extent, cognitive constriction and premature closure account for why many problems that cripple relationships appear so intractable. After all, if you can't even think of a solution, you're not likely to cope effectively in eliminating or reducing the severity of the problem.

To counteract this effect of stress, you and your partner will brainstorm alternative solutions until you both feel satisfied that you have exhausted *all* possibilities—including ideas that, at first blush, appear farfetched, foolish, or even impossible.

Only when you have completed the brainstorming and made a list of every possible solution will you embark on Step Four— a systematic evaluation of the pros and cons of each. Take each alternative, one at a time, and discuss the benefits and drawbacks of putting the alternative into action.

In Step Five, review your evaluations and *select one solution*.

Remember, the intrinsic quality of a knotty problem is that the solution is difficult. Thus, there may not be any one alternative that stands out as the obvious best thing to do. But you still must select.

Next, in Step Six, you must *act* on your selection. Work out a plan to put your proposed solution into practice. Then, implement your plan. Without this critical step, problem solving will not occur.

Finally, after a week or two, you will complete the problem-solving process by beginning it again from the top. In other words, you will evaluate how your solution is working and attempt to identify whatever new problems or "wrinkles" may have developed that require smoothing out and reconsideration.

The Seven Step Solution is an invaluable tool. By successfully targeting, solving, and ultimately eliminating your problems, you will purge your relationship of harmful toxins and stress.

3. Behavior-change contracts. This technique is designed to eliminate two major irritants from your relationship: something your partner is doing (or failing to do) that is causing you to feel toxic emotions, and something you are doing (or failing to do) that is causing your partner to react with negative feelings. The inventory you completed in exercise 1 in this chapter allowed you to identify at least five such offending behaviors in your partner as well as in yourself.

Each of you should identify a behavior in the other that you would like to see altered or stopped. The sole criterion for qualifying a behavior as a target for change is that one of you reacts negatively.

In formulating your request, it is important that you attempt to describe what your partner is *doing* rather than how he or she is *being*. For example, instead of saying, "Stop being cold and rejecting," *describe* your partner's cold and rejecting behavior. You might say, "It hurts me and makes me feel angry when you roll over in bed, face away from me, and move as far as possible to your side of the bed." By sticking to concrete descriptions, your partner can focus specifically on the behavior that upsets you, and both of you can better judge whether, in fact, the offending actions change.

In addition, you must describe to your partner as accurately and precisely as possible the nature of the negative feelings evoked by the offending behavior. Instead of saying, for example, "You make me feel bad," you should say, "That behavior makes me feel undesirable and ugly. Then, I get depressed and angry."

The next step in the exercise is the key to its success. You will not stop with merely asking your partner to cease the behavior that bothers you. Rather, you will go the extra distance and help your partner figure out what could be done that might make you feel better.

It is vital that you work together in developing an alternative or substitute to take the place of the offending behavior.

After you and your partner have conducted an analysis of the problematic and substitute actions for both of you, you should proceed to devising a *behavioral contract*. This means that *both* of you will agree to change your behavior according to the prescriptions you have developed.

Each of you should have the opportunity to exact a promise from the other to change a behavior that has become a source of unhappiness or irritation. Keep in mind, however, that behavior change generally does not happen quickly or easily. You should expect "slips"—times when either of you may regress to your old ways. On those occasions, a gentle reminder will be far more effective and less damaging to the relationship than will an explosion of anger, however righteous the complaint.

If your behavior-change contracts have yielded positive results, remember to reinforce your partner for his or her efforts. Words of appreciation, praise, and recognition are as important in shaping and molding the behavior of adults as they are in the rearing of children or pets. Positive reinforcement strengthens desired responses and increases the probability that the new and improved behaviors will soon become ingrained replacements for the problematic actions.

4. Reentry time. For many toxic relationships, the time when partners reconnect after a period of normal, daily separation can produce volatile emotions. Typically, the stresses and pressures of the day build up, and each partner becomes a target of the other's displaced hostility. Because they no longer function as sources of support and comfort to each other, partners in toxic relationships often view each other merely as additional sources of demand or as potent irritants. And, because neither partner gets from the relationship that which he or she sorely needs emotionally, the period of reconnection frequently elicits strong feelings of frustration, which then trigger a host of other negative emotions.

For most couples, the reconnection comes at the end of the workday when the partners arrive home. If both partners work, there is generally little time or opportunity to make the transition from the work mode to a more relaxed, social mode of interaction. Consequently, working partners often bounce their stress off each other, with the result that the stress of each is greatly magnified.

For couples where only one partner—typically the male—works outside the home, the reconnection again usually comes at the end of the day. This time, however, the respective rhythms of the partners are likely to be quite different. For example, in a traditional family, the man brings home the stresses and pressures of the adult world while the woman—if she is a homemaker—is affected by the stress of managing the demands of children and the home.

This exercise is designed to help you develop a transitional reentry time that diffuses negative emotions. Your purpose is to invent a reentry ritual that will serve you both better than the way in which you are now reconnecting.

Perhaps, for example, you now greet your partner at the front door and follow him or her with a recounting of your day and your troubles. Perhaps, on the other hand, moments after seeing you, your partner presents you with a litany of criticisms—things that you have done wrong or failed to do altogether.

You need to become aware of just how you and your partner typically reconnect. You must assess whether the reconnection time is a source or trigger of negative emotions. If the process is troublesome for one partner, it should be considered a problem for both.

Ask yourself what kind of transition time between your daily obligations or activities and your interaction with your partner you would most like to have. Perhaps you need an hour to be alone, to read your mail, or to take a brief nap or hot bath; maybe you need to exercise vigorously or just sit quietly with the newspaper.

On the other hand, you may be desperate for adult conversation by the end of the day; or you may need to be hugged, kissed, and calmed down. Or, perhaps you are primed and ready to play and talk with your children—to help them with their homework or roll around on the floor roughhousing.

The point is that people vary widely in terms of what they

most want and need in order to make the most comfortable, pleasant transition from their workday to their personal lives. One of the biggest problems couples have is that their transition preferences clash. Where one wants quiet time alone, the other craves company and conversation; where one desires cuddling and a cocktail, the other needs a five-mile jog. The challenge, of course, is to reconnect in a way that your respective needs are met and that doesn't occasion an outburst of negative emotions.

When each of you has identified your preferred reentry style, determine whether a compatible solution emerges. Generally, with creativity and cooperation, a new, ritualized, pleasant reentry time can be developed.

You may well need to experiment and alternate with different reentry methods; continual improvements and adjustments are almost invariably required. The key element of this technique is that you both commit yourselves to breaking old patterns. Once you identify clearly what the triggers of negativity are in your reconnection time, your goal is to remove those triggers. The reconnection can only become better when you have found a way to meet your mutual reentry needs.

5. Time Out. Negative emotions are evoked by patterns of provocative behavior. These patterns of dangerous dancing are well-rehearsed sequences of action and reaction, usually fueled by anger and frustration. In turn, the provocative behavior produces more toxic emotions, which sustain and aggravate the escalating cycle.

Excising negative emotions from your relationship, then, requires a mechanism by which your dangerous dancing patterns can be interrupted and eventually broken. The following technique, called "Time Out," will effectively derail the action/ reaction sequence, thereby stopping the negative emotional consequences.

Knowing when to call Time Out requires that you and your partner develop an awareness of the cues that signal your dangerous dances. Make an explicit agreement with each other to purge your relationship of dangerous behavioral patterns that lead to negative emotions. Agree further that you will honor your partner's request, at any time, for a Time Out period without resistance or argument.

This is how the Time Out mechanism works: Whenever you feel yourself starting to react negatively to something your partner is doing, ask for a five-minute break from the interaction. If possible, separate yourself physically by going to a different room or area. If you can't maneuver around the environment—for example, if you are in a car—you will have to take Time Out by merely remaining silent for five minutes. However, the best method, if possible, is literally to get away from each other for the Time Out period.

Time Out is intended to break your ingrained reaction pattern. This is easily accomplished by engaging your mind in an irrelevant but somewhat demanding mental exercise such as counting backward from seventy-three by fives. The purpose is to stop your mind from proceeding along the path of negative feeling and action upon which it has embarked. Do this relatively slowly; focus on regulating your breathing as you count until you are inhaling in a relaxed, deep manner and exhaling slowly and completely. The breathing will calm you; the mental exercise will distract you from the negative interaction that you have just left.

Then, return your thoughts to the issue at hand. Examine your reactions to your partner's behavior. Try to recall what set off the argument or negative pattern. Sometimes, when the dangerous dancing escalates, neither person can even remember the original cause of the problem. If you cannot bring to mind what started your reaction, consider the possibility that, whatever it was, it isn't important enough to poison your relationship.

The most important thing is that you use Time Out to *regain control*.

6. Choose Your Fights. This technique is for partners in toxic relationships who fight often and repetitively about the same issues. In toxic relationships, people often fight merely out of habit.

Since arguments are emotionally taxing and draining, they should be engaged in very selectively and then only as a means to resolve a conflict. The criterion for choosing to fight over any specific issue should rest with your subjective judgment of how important, meaningful, or tied to deeper values the matter truly is.

Conflicts generally are destructive when communication is decreased, strategies of threat and coercion are used, fundamental values that hold the relationship together are called into question, and no viable resolution is reached. Consequently, the stage is set for repetitive conflicts over the same or similar issues in the future.

In healthy relationships, periodic conflicts still occur. However, the manner of handling them is constructive in that it serves the long-term interests of the relationship. Both partners adopt an attitude of flexibility and genuine willingness to negotiate for the sake of the relationship rather than try to "win" at any cost. Finally, constructive conflicts lead to a viable resolution that precludes future conflicts about the same issue.

To apply the rule of Choose Your Fights, you must learn to become sensitive to the signals that a conflict is beginning; perhaps certain "signal" words or phrases are used, such as, "That really makes me angry," or, "I can't believe you did that—you better have a damn good explanation!"

You and your partner must agree to follow the Choose Your Fights rule. Whenever either one of you senses that an argument is about to ensue, an appeal to Choose Your Fights should be made. If you sense that an argument over where to go for dinner, for example, is about to break out, you might say, "Wait a minute. Let's choose our fights. Is this something we really want to fight about?"

Then, take a few moments to consider the question. If the answer is a mutual no, then the motivation should exist for resolving the issue immediately. If the decision to fight is made by one partner but not the other, a conflict is still likely to be aborted. This is because it takes two to tangle, and if one is really not willing to fight about an issue, the other can't very well fight alone. When you both determine that the issue merits an argument, you can proceed with the knowledge that the matter has significant meaning and importance to both partners.

If you choose to fight, make every effort to conform your behavior to the guidelines of constructive conflict. Be sure that the flow of information is increased rather than decreased. This means no silent treatments or verbal devices to foil conversation, such as, "I don't even feel like talking to you anymore," or, "What's the point in talking? You never understand anything anyway." Use the occasion of conflict as an opportunity to explain your feelings about things that you may not otherwise have discussed. Work toward a goal of understanding your partner's position thoroughly and having your partner understand yours.

Be conscious of maintaining flexibility and a willingness to negotiate. Being willing to fight doesn't mean being determined to win the argument at all costs. Take care to keep the discussion confined to the issue at hand, without generalizing and questioning the fundamental values that hold your bond together.

For example, if you are arguing about money, keep the discussion confined to financial issues. Make every attempt to avoid such accusations as claiming that your partner must not love you if he or she spends money that way, or that you cannot trust your partner because of money. Bringing fundamental values such as love or trust into the arena of conflict will have a destructive, sabotaging effect on your relationship that will estrange you and your partner and move you farther away from a workable, cooperative solution.

If you both have chosen to fight about a specific issue, work toward a constructive resolution. Do not use the issue as a vehicle for launching attacks on each other's character or for spewing forth long-suppressed profanities or expletives, or for name-calling. These indulgences serve to escalate the conflict and to obstruct a resolution.

Finally, focus your conflict on this goal: How can you avoid having this same argument or similar ones in the future? Try to develop some rules or standing agreements that will obviate the need to have the same fight again.

7. Negative Thought Stopping. A central axiom of modern psychology is that the way you think creates your moods. Distorted negative thinking is believed to lie at the core of depressed moods; exaggerated, extreme, and unrealistic thinking is the cognitive basis for anxiety.

Since thoughts create emotions, the direct elimination of negative thoughts can be expected to eliminate or, at minimum, greatly reduce toxic emotions.

But, how do you stop thoughts? While this may sound like a tall order, there is a highly effective yet simple method for eliminating negative thoughts. The method comes from the tradition of behavior modification (remember, thinking is a form of behavior) and is actually called *Thought Stopping*.

First, identify the specific thoughts that trigger your negative emotions. Over the course of one week, take careful note of your feelings. At four specific times each day—9:00 A.M., noon, 3:00 P.M., and 9:00 P.M.—ask yourself what kind of negative emotions you have experienced since your last notation (e.g., anger, anxiety, sadness, self-loathing, frustration). You should pay particular attention to the toxic emotions you have felt in response to your partner or another person with whom you have a troublesome or poisonous relationship.

Write down, as descriptively as possible, the negative feelings you can recall. Then, for each emotion, try to remember what was happening right before you began having the feeling and/or while you were experiencing it. This allows you to mentally recreate the situation out of which your negative feelings developed.

Next, write down what you were thinking in response to the situations you described. Do not censor your recorded thoughts in any way; nobody will read this journal except you, and it is imperative that you discover the content of your thoughts by writing down as faithfully as possible what went on in your mind. Your goal is to identify the trigger thought of your negative emotions. For example, "When Brian asked Mary to present the report instead of me, I thought, 'I'm no good at this job. . . . I'm never the one chosen. . . . I'll probably fail at this job and get fired. I feel so inferior to Mary.' "

The Negative Thought Stopping technique is designed to interrupt and ultimately rid you of the thoughts that cause your negative emotions. By learning to regulate your thoughts, you will greatly increase your sense of control. Since you cannot directly change the behavior of others—nor should you even try to do so—this method provides you with something that you *can* do to change the way you feel. In effect, it means that you will learn to respond differently to situations and/or behaviors that have upset you in the past by altering your cognitive reactions.

After keeping your journal for one week, you will have a good sense of which negative thoughts fill your mind most frequently and therefore contribute most often to your negative feelings. Choose one specific thought from your record to target for change.

First, fill your mind with the negative thought pattern. For example, start worrying, or make negative predictions or self-devaluing comments. Next, close your eyes and visualize a traffic stop sign. Use your mind's eye to conjure the image of an eight-sided, red sign with large white letters that spell S-T-O-P.

Keep focusing on the stop sign. Now, imagine that you are walking backward, away from the sign, to a distance of about twenty feet. See the letters getting smaller as you move farther away from the sign. Next, visualize yourself walking up so close to the sign that your nose is virtually touching it. See the blur of whiteness in front of you without clear definition of the individual letters because you are so close. Then, move back again until you can see the "STOP" very clearly.

Using your mind's eye like a camera lens, take the "STOP" out of focus and make it blurred. Then, refocus the lens until the letters are crystal clear. Note the clarity and sharpness of your mind's lens. Maintain the image of the stop sign for ten more seconds, counting slowly, saying, "One—I've stopped my thought; two—I've stopped my thought," and so on.

By the count of ten, or long before, you will realize that the negative trigger thought has disappeared from your mind. This is because your mind cannot engage in the imagery task while maintaining the content of the trigger thought. By distracting yourself with mental imagery and using the message of "STOP," you will have gained control of the cognitive process that produces your toxic feelings.

As you become more proficient at Negative Thought Stopping, you will begin to experience a sense of relaxation and relief at aborting a negative emotional reaction. The imagery, of course, will not make the behavior or situation that originally upset you go away. But it will help you gain control of the spiraling thoughts that create and reinforce your negative response.

These methods comprise the purging approach to detoxification. The remaining treatment, to which we turn in the next chapter, is neutralizing negative emotions through the use of behavioral antidotes.

18

How to Detoxify Your Relationship

III. Techniques for Neutralizing Toxic Emotions

The last approach to detoxification is the administration of behavioral antidotes designed to *neutralize* your emotional poisons. Negative emotions will be counteracted by the substitution of behaviors and thoughts that are incompatible with the toxins.

Psychologically, the human mind cannot and will not long sustain a particular feeling in the presence of an incongruous feeling, thought, or action. The reason for this is called *cognitive dissonance*—an uncomfortable tension that occurs whenever mental incongruities exist. You have probably recognized that you are uncomfortable when your thoughts do not jibe with your behavior; or when your feelings and behavior do not square up with your thoughts. This reaction is inherent in everyone's psychological wiring.

When a feeling and a behavior are incompatible, a drive develops to change one or the other in order to bring them into consonance. Only then will the tension of incongruity be alleviated.

You will apply the principle of cognitive dissonance in the techniques that follow in order to neutralize your toxic emotions. By engaging in actions designed to be incongruous or incompatible with your negative emotions, you will actually force those emotions to change.

1. Relaxation, exercise, and laughter as antidotes. Many of the most dangerous toxic emotions in relationships can be neutralized by relaxing, exercising, and/or laughing. Cognitive dissonance makes it virtually impossible to feel anxious and relaxed at the same time. Similarly, hostility, cynicism, and anger can be neutralized by laughter, as well as by the stress reduction that comes from vigorous physical exercise. Feelings of loss of control and, to some extent, low self-esteem also are counteracted by relaxation and exercise.

You will need a repertoire of activities to help you achieve relaxation, exercise, and laughter. Select at least one activity from each of the categories below to design your personal program. Of course, you may use as many activities within each category as you want, and you may certainly develop methods of your own. The important thing is that you have specific techniques to help you relax, exercise, and laugh.

A. EXERCISE

- Walk at a moderate pace for twenty to thirty minutes, on the street, a jogging track, or a treadmill.
- Jog for twenty to thirty minutes.
- Jump rope for ten minutes.
- Do twenty to thirty minutes of aerobics, calisthenics, or free-form dance.
- Use a Stairmaster or ascend and descend a staircase for five minutes.
- Ride a stationary or regular bike for twenty to thirty minutes.

B. RELAXATION

- Lie on a bed or sofa, close your eyes, and inhale through your nose deeply and slowly to the count of five; hold your breath for two seconds, then exhale slowly through your mouth to the count of five. Continue this rhythmic breathing for ten minutes. Feel your arms, legs, hands, head, and torso progressively growing warm and heavy as you become more and more relaxed.
- Lie in a warm bath or hot tub for ten to fifteen minutes; listen to mellow, relaxing music while you soak; turn the lights down or off and illuminate the area with soft candlelight.
- Sit in a sauna or steam room for five to ten minutes; close your eyes and feel the tension leaving your body as you perspire.
- Get a massage.

C. LAUGHTER

- Play an audio or videotape of your favorite comedian in concert.
- Go to a funny movie or rent a video of a good comedy film.
- Read a humor book, joke collection, or amusing magazine article.
- Think about some of the funniest things that have ever happened to you; write them down in a very humorous way and then tell your stories to a friend; try to reexperience your original amusement.

To use exercise, relaxation, or laughter (or a combination) as an antidote to toxic feelings, you need only identify the onset of a negative emotion and, as quickly as possible, engage in one of the behaviors listed above or any other that you have devised to achieve the same result.

In selecting the type of antidote, consider which emotion you are feeling. Choose an activity that seems most incongruous or incompatible with your negative emotion. As you engage in the prescribed antidote activity, attempt to clear your mind of the disturbing feelings. Concentrate instead on feeling relaxed, invigorated, or amused. Let the toxic emotion recede to the background of your consciousness. When you have finished your antidote activity, you will discover that the intensity of the negative emotion has decreased significantly or disappeared altogether.

If after a short period of time the negativity begins to return, you may either repeat the antidote activity or try to recall the positive feelings you had when you were engaged in it.

2. Visualization exercises. This method takes advantage of your mind's potent capacity for producing mental imagery. The power of visual imagery is so great that your mind and body often respond as though they were exposed to the real rather than to the imagined event.

In toxic relationships, people often feel the desire to escape to a place where they would be free of worries, aggravation, harassment, pressure, and other irritations. While escape is rarely possible in reality, it is entirely attainable with visual imagery.

There are three specific images that function best to counteract toxic emotions: a scene that connotes peace and serenity; a scene that connotes security and safety; and a scene that connotes pride and high self-esteem.

To develop your visual imagery scenarios, you will need to write a highly personalized script, tailored to your needs and tastes. First, write a few paragraphs, with as much detail as possible, of a scene that evokes feelings of peacefulness, serenity, and calmness. Perhaps it is a beautiful mountain scene with a flowing stream and lovely wildlife; maybe it is a sailboat on calm, blue waters; or your scene might be lying on a beach, basking in the sun on a vacation. It can be anything in your imagination that connotes peacefulness and calm.

Your script should be written in the first person, present tense, and begin, "I am sitting [or standing or looking] . . ." You may include another person in your script, provided he or she contributes to your sense of peacefulness.

Next, write a few paragraphs to describe a second scene that evokes feelings of security and safety. This time your scene might be an actual recollection of something from your childhood that was especially reassuring. Or it might be a fantasy of a scene that you have never experienced but believe would have the desired comforting effect on you.

Finally, write your third script for a scene that evokes feelings of mastery, pride, and high self-esteem. This time you will need to recall or invent an image of yourself achieving a desired goal, being lauded by others for your accomplishments, winning a competition, or reaching a particular aim of physical appearance, such as a desired weight. Again, the content is designed only for *you*. The sole purpose is that when *you* visualize the scene, *you* have feelings of enhanced self-esteem.

The next step is to record your three scenarios onto an audio cassette. Read each of your scripts onto a tape, using a relatively slow, mellow voice. In effect, you will be producing an effective self-hypnosis tape. When you want to elicit a certain feeling, you need only select one of your three scenarios, turn on your tape, lie down, close your eyes, and visualize the scene. The tape will aid you to conjure up a distinct visual image. After the tape stops, you should continue your visualization for a period of at least ten minutes. Merely continue seeing in your mind the scene that evokes the desired antidote feelings.

You may use your visualization tape whenever negative emotions strike. Select the most specific antidote script to counteract the emotions with which you are struggling.

For example, if you feel hostile or angry, your best antidote would be the scenario that evokes peacefulness. If your predominant negative emotion is anxiety or fear, you would need the safety and security visualization. When your self-esteem is low, try the scenario that makes you feel better about yourself.

3. Wearing rose-colored glasses. Negative emotions have a distorting effect on the way you process and interpret events. Depression and unhappiness create a gray, obscuring fog that darkens your vision of everything in your life—even the best parts of it. Negative moods can also make your future outlook seem hopeless and grim.

If in reality you were walking around wearing gray-colored glasses and consequently seeing your world as a gloomy place, the obvious remedy would be to wear rose-colored or, at least, clear lenses. In the same way, a corrective antidote for the distorting, negative effects of toxic emotions on your world-view is to wear imaginary, psychologically rose-colored glasses.

Although your toxic relationship by definition creates negativity, you may well be viewing your problems as far worse than they actually are. Your negative emotions predispose you to look for the negative things about your partner and your relationship while overlooking or discounting positive aspects.

The rose-colored glasses antidote is rather easily accomplished given the right mindset, adequate discipline, and a little imagination. When you arise in the morning, imagine that you are donning special, magical glasses that allow you to see everything in the best possible light.

Of course, the rose-colored lenses are only in your mind's eye and therefore not visible to others. Imagine further that you are now able to screen out the negative features of your emotional and physical environment and to make the positive features salient and particularly appealing.

Wear the glasses for an entire day and keep a journal to record your experiences. When you see other people, especially those with whom you associate negative emotions, take special note of their best qualities, look for their relative strengths, and do your best to overlook their weaknesses and minimize their shortcomings.

Walk around your home taking pleasure in the pretty things you see—the light through a window, the color of a throw pillow, the warmth and coziness of a room. Look in the mirror and let the magical lenses screen out the negative things you usually see about yourself. Pay attention to the most attractive things about your appearance and note them in your journal.

Throughout the day, continue searching for the best things in your relationships, in other people, and in your surroundings. Your imaginary lenses will serve as a potent antidote when you turn them to an examination of your toxic relationship. With a rose-colored psyche, you will not see people's faults or read into their actions bad intentions and malice toward you. For the day, then, you may be somewhat unprotected emotionally; but the gains in counteracting your usually negative perceptions will be worth the temporary exposure. Your purpose is not to become distorted in the other direction as a Pollyanna or cockeyed optimist. Rather, your intent should be to balance and correct the negative bias caused by your toxic relationship.

Use the rose-colored glasses whenever you feel overwhelmed or unbalanced by negativity. Assume that your bad mood and negative emotions have skewed your perception and that an antidote to neutralize the bias will help.

4. The social-support antidote. Social support is a consistent correlate of good health. Being around other people—especially people who care about you and provide you with unconditional support and love—is among the best antidotes for all toxic emotions. Family bonds, for example, can be very healing, provided that the relationships are fundamentally healthy and not the source of toxicity in the first place. Family offers the benefit of people who have known you all your life and with whom you share history, values, and, often, strengths and vulnerabilities.

If at least some of your family relationships are healthy, work on strengthening and nurturing them. Attend get-togethers whenever possible, and be an initiator of family activities.

Many families fall into ruts of the same old ritualized Sunday dinners or holiday feasts. While these are important, look for creative ways to celebrate other family occasions.

Ideally, families are the very essence of social-support systems and, as such, can offer comfort and solace during times of pain, loss, and difficulty. If you do not presently turn to members of your family for emotional support, make some efforts in that direction, and offer your support in reciprocation.

Friends, too, are invaluable sources of social support. Being there for your friends when they go through difficult periods will benefit you as well as them because feeling needed and helping those about whom you care is inherently satisfying and good for your health, too. Although you should not perform acts of kindness with the expectation of getting them in return, the fact is that you probably will.

By maintaining several high-quality relationships in your life with family members and friends, you will be less vulnerable to involvement in an addictive relationship. Multiple satisfying emotional relationships from which you derive satisfaction and positive input to your self-esteem lessen your overdependency on one relationship as the total measure of your self-worth.

In addition to the antidote properties of social support, receiving positive emotions from several significant relationships serves to dilute the toxic effects of one. In other words, by spreading your emotional eggs around to a handful of relationship baskets, the impact of one bond turning toxic will be far less devastating.

5. Practicing your religious faith. Another correlate of physical health and self-healing emotions is religious faith. If you are a spiritual person, availing yourself of the benefits of practicing your faith is a powerful antidote to toxic emotions.

If you and your partner are of the same religion, practicing your faith together may help neutralize some of the toxic feelings between you. In particular, the antidotes of love and forgiveness are pervasive themes in sermons and religious liturgy.

Strengthening your faith will help to counteract hopelessness, depression, anxiety, helplessness, and loss of control. In addition, organized religions offer strong social-support systems to both individuals and couples.

6. Building self-esteem. Improving your self-concept and self-esteem serves as a strong antidote to toxic emotions. When you feel good about yourself, you are better able to take on the challenge of difficult problems. If your self-esteem is strong, a general spillover effect occurs into many other areas of your life and relationships: You feel more in control, more hopeful, less vulnerable, less anxious, and certainly less helpless.

There are several avenues that lead to better self-esteem. First, you can focus on the superficial yet important aspect of your physical appearance. If you are overweight, for example, going on an effective diet and exercise program will work wonders for your sense of control; successfully losing weight will contribute to a sense of self-worth. When you look and feel better, you will expect to be treated better by others. This rise in your expectations will motivate you to improve your damaged relationships.

In addition to losing (or gaining) weight and getting into better physical shape, you might need to focus on sharpening up your wardrobe, improving your overall grooming, getting a new hairstyle, pampering yourself with a manicure, pedicure, and/or facial, or coloring your hair to cover gray if it bothers you.

Your self-esteem also will rise if you acquire a new skill or develop an additional area of knowledge. For example, you can study a foreign language, take up a new sport, or try your hand at painting or ceramics. Learning something new pays off by providing a sense of mastery, which in turn augments your general sense of control in life. When you rise to the challenge of learning something new, you will be able to confront other challenges more successfully.

Your damaged self-esteem can be repaired, in part, by taking an inventory of your best qualities instead of focusing on your flaws. One negative effect of your toxic relationship probably has been to dampen your sense of self-worth by distorting your assessment of your personal assets.

Make a list of all your positive qualities—personality traits, physical features, talents, interests, and so on. Because your negative mindset may preclude you from making an accurate or comprehensive list, adopt the perspective of someone who knows and loves you, such as a best friend or close relative. Try to see yourself the way he or she sees you. You might even review your assets list with that person. Ask if there are additional positive qualities about yourself that you have omitted. Explicitly counting your good points will help correct your distorted sense of self-worth and neutralize your toxic emotions.

Of course, solidifying good self-esteem is a process that requires sustaining positive behaviors over time and acquiring deeper self-knowledge and self-acceptance. But these three approaches—improving personal appearance, acquiring new skills, and developing an assets list—are effective ways to start building your self-esteem *now*.

Maintenance of Gains and Positive Reinforcement

You now have learned numerous ways to detoxify your relationship. The effectiveness of these techniques will depend on your commitment to use them on an ongoing basis, and to sustain your motivation even when your progress is sometimes slow.

Whatever gains you make in building positive rewards, purging negative feelings, and neutralizing toxic emotions, it is imperative that you keep two concepts foremost in your mind and that you put them into practice:

Concept #1: In order to stay healthy, positive, and rewarding, your *relationship's functioning must be continually maintained.* Think of your newly detoxified relationship as equivalent to a sleek, finely tuned sports car that was temporarily broken down. Imagine further that you have been working on the car for some time and now it is running like a dream.

You know enough about a fussy high-performance car to recognize its need for constant maintenance in order to keep it purring at its peak level. Unfortunately, though, most people don't recognize this critically important feature of relationships. They mistakenly assume that if a relationship is running well, it doesn't require any attention or work. Instead, they wait until the relationship breaks down before they attend to it.

But a fine relationship, like a sleek sports car, is equally demanding of continual attention and maintenance. Your hard efforts will pay off amply in the smooth, satisfying functioning of your relationship. And the maintenance work can be something you actually learn to love doing.

Maintenance work on a relationship consists of keeping your rewards high and your costs down. This means that you and your partner need to have a regular time to review how things are going. Don't focus only on problems—although these certainly are important; acknowledge the good things as well. Ask yourselves what can be done to create positive interactions more often and what can be done to keep the rewards high.

Problems represent the costs. Deal with problems as soon as they arise, before they fester and become poisonous again. You now have the skills to solve problems together and methods to rid your relationship of other bothersome costs as well.

Don't minimize problems. If something bothers you, it's important enough to discuss and certainly significant enough to resolve. Avoid dismissing or discounting things that bother you and always acknowledge any problems raised by your partner.

On the other hand, don't catastrophize, either. Problems do not have to become overwhelming or crisis-sized in proportion. If you see them that way, you are probably experiencing the distorting effects of depression or anxiety. Once your relationship is successfully detoxified, few if any problems intrinsic to your relationship will become truly huge in size or escalate into real crises. Even then, with your healthy, supportive relationship, you will be able to face together the inevitable stresses and problems that life entails.

Concept #2: Never forget the value of *positive reinforcement.* People readily acknowledge how important it is for children to be encouraged and rewarded and for dogs to get pats on the head and biscuits for good behavior. All too often, though, the strong need that adults also have to be positively reinforced for their efforts is overlooked.

Relationships falter when they function only on negative reinforcement (e.g., nagging, criticism) and punishment. Relationships, and the people in them, thrive on being positively reinforced for what is good and right about them.

There are many forms of meaningful positive reinforcement. Principal among them are verbal modes (e.g., "I really appreciate what you did for me," or, "I love you a lot") and gestures of physical affection. Thoughtful notes, funny cards, gifts, and special surprises offer an element of spontaneity, pleasure, and fun while providing the reinforcement necessary to keep the relationship healthy and happy.

The importance of supplying and deriving pleasure and fun from your relationship cannot be too strongly emphasized. Unfortunately, too many adults—especially those in unhappy relationships—have actually forgotten how to have fun. So, we turn now to a quick lesson in putting fun and pleasure back into your relationship.

19

Building Fun and Pleasure into
Your Relationship

People who are in chronically unhappy relationships often become inured to their pain and distress. They may even come to believe that all relationships inevitably cause suffering and that the best they can hope for is temporary relief from their misery.

This low expectation is more a product of depression than a reflection of realistic thinking. In fact, a rewarding, healthy relationship goes far beyond just the absence of pain. A good relationship consistently delivers pleasure while also keeping painful experiences at a minimum.

Think of a scale that ranges from -10 to zero and then up to $+10$ as representing the full range of emotional experiences in any relationship. The negative range indicates painful, distressing, toxic emotions; zero represents neutral, essentially flat emotions; and the plus numbers reflect the upper range of positive feelings and opportunities for pleasure that a relationship might yield.

Earlier, as you tackled the challenge of detoxifying your

negative relationship, you were probably most concerned with getting out of your immediate pain. That usually is the short-term goal of people caught in the struggle of toxic emotions, and it is a necessary, valid goal.

But reaching only the neutral point on the continuum of relationship experience—escaping pain—is not a sufficient goal to meet the criterion of a healthy, rewarding relationship. After you detoxify your relationship, your second aim should be to move it into the realm of *pleasure*. Positive, pleasurable emotions benefit your physical and mental health, and the momentum they create sustains the motivation necessary to continue to improve the quality of your relationship.

The most direct access to the positive side of the continuum is to build opportunities for fun, pleasure, playfulness, and humor into your relationship. Sharing fun and pleasurable experiences with your partner helps create more positive associations relative to the relationship generally. This is true simply because you tend to like people with whom you have fun; and you also are likely to attribute other positive qualities to your partner if he or she provides you with pleasure.

Sharing laughter, fun, and pleasure with your partner will strengthen your emotional bond and incline you both toward fonder feelings. When you are capable of having fun together and generating pleasure for and with each other, there will be greater motivation to keep the relationship functioning smoothly so that more fun and pleasure can be experienced in the future.

But, since your relationship has been toxic, you must re-learn—or perhaps learn for the first time—how to have fun together. The techniques in this chapter will help you move your relationship into the pleasure zone.

What Is Your Daily Fun Level?

The initial step in building pleasure into your relationship is to become aware of how much—or how little—fun and pleasure you currently experience.

Each day for the next two weeks, make a rating of how much fun you have had. Use the continuum described earlier as your personal fun-rating scale: The range goes from −10, meaning the most awful day with the least amount of fun possible, up to +10, meaning the most wonderful day with the greatest amount of fun possible. Do your daily evaluation in the evening, preferably at the same time each night.

After you have rated your fun level, indicate what percentage of your total waking time was spent in the company of your partner. This will allow you to see at a glance the correlation between your fun level and time spent with your partner. Your ultimate goal is to make the correlation high and positive. In other words, you are working toward high fun ratings when you have spent a lot of time together. However, this doesn't mean that your time apart should be miserable. On the contrary, if your time away from each other also is pleasant, you will both be in a better state of mind to be together when you reconnect. However, time together optimally should be time treasured for the pleasure it produces. Even daily tasks, such as household chores or child-rearing responsibilities, can take on a dimension of fun if you find ways to entertain or amuse each other while you work.

The third component of your rating is to identify the obstacles that are blocking or inhibiting your ability to have fun. Perhaps you are under too much stress or you feel too anxious. Maybe you and your partner are regressing into hostility or conflict. Or perhaps you just haven't taken the time or made the effort to build more fun into your day. By identifying which people, things, or feelings are getting in the way of your fun, you will be in a position to remove the obstacles.

After two weeks, you should have a good sense of your fun level and how your relationship either contributes to or detracts from it. And you will better understand your overall patterns— such as having fun on weekends but none on weekdays, for example.

The daily ratings will provide a *baseline* level from which you

can improve and against which you can compare your progress.

After the two-week initial rating period, you should discuss
your rating scores and obstacle identification with your partner.

Pleasurable Activities Menu

If you have been plagued by toxic emotions, particularly depression, you may not even be able to think of things that
would be fun and pleasurable. This is a common complaint of
unhappy people.

Again, you must understand that your seeming inability to
think of fun or pleasurable things to do is a symptom of your
problem rather than a reflection of reality. There *are* many ways
to have fun and many pleasurable things to do.

All you need is a menu from which to select activities. To be
most effective and meaningful, the pleasurable activities list
should be developed with your partner. Working jointly, make
a list of at least twenty things that you could do together that
would be pleasurable, fun, humorous, or playful. Make your
list as varied as possible. Include activities that you currently
do—or used to do—as well as new things that you would like
to try. Your list should include activities that can be accomplished in a very short period of time—as little as five or ten
minutes—as well as more time-consuming involvements. Include activities that are free as well as those that require an
expenditure of money. Naturally, you should add new activities to the list whenever you think of them.

In addition to the joint activities, each of you should develop
an independent list of at least ten pleasurable things to do
alone or with someone other than your partner. Again, be sure
to vary the time required, the cost involved, and the familiarity
versus novelty of the activities; and add to the list whenever
you can.

If you get stuck on either your joint or your independent list, ask for suggestions from friends and relatives. Find out what other people do together for fun.

Peak Experiences

This exercise should be done independently, so that the results can be compared to your partner's and discussed. You will be looking back in time, over the entire history of your relationship, to identify the peak experiences of fun, pleasure, and laughter that you have enjoyed together.

List the five most pleasurable, fun-filled, and/or delight-provoking experiences you have ever had with your partner. Review your answers together and try to reexperience some of the feelings you had during those peak times in your relationship. Now circle those experiences that you would like to repeat, assuming it is possible to do so. Perhaps none of your peak memories are of things you could do again; or, you may be unwilling to spoil or sully your fondest memories by risking disappointment in a replay.

However, some of your recollections might stimulate ideas for things you used to enjoy doing together that have just dropped out of your repertoire and could easily be reincorporated. Additionally, you should use the peak experience list as material for your pleasurable activities menu in the preceding exercise.

By comparing your memories of peak pleasure to your partner's, you will learn where your memories coincide and where they do not. Use the opportunity to discuss your feelings so that you better understand what gives your partner pleasure and so that your preferences are clearly understood in return.

The Pleasurable Activities Regimen

Three changes will make a measurable difference in your daily fun ratings and overall happiness. First, you must remove as many obstacles as possible that may be blocking your ability to have fun. Run any problems through the Seven Step Solution and do what needs to be done to eliminate the things blocking your pleasure.

Next, a shift in your outlook and mindset will enhance the pleasure you obtain from your normal daily activities. Think about the fact that people who laugh, feel pleasure, and have fun enjoy better health and a far higher quality of life than do those whose lives are bereft of festivity. So, letting yourself have more fun will affect something as fundamental as your very survival.

The survival and viability of your relationship also depend on having fun and experiencing pleasure together. Without those elements, you will merely exist together, living, at best, in the neutral zone of experience. You can and should expect more out of your relationship than that.

Feeling pleasure and having fun are largely states of mind. It is necessary that you shift your perspective so that you look for the opportunities every day to increase your pleasure level.

The final change is the most important: *You have to behave differently*. You must do things together that will involve laughter, playfulness, fun, and pleasure. You must also do things independently that are fun. Commit yourself to making time to have fun just as you do to work. Since your health depends on it, fun is serious business.

You and your partner can begin moving into the pleasure zone immediately by doing at least one pleasurable activity together each weekday and at least four each weekend. Select activities from your independent lists to augment your fun together. Choose your joint activities from both lists—yours and your partner's. The important thing is simply that you *do* them.

As soon as you begin your pleasurable activities regimen, start your rating exercise again. Indicate your daily fun rating, the percentage of time spent together, and the obstacles blocking your enjoyment. Review your ratings together on a weekly basis. Discover the activities that yield the highest fun scores for both of you, and work together to remove hindrances to your fun.

Compare your current weekly average fun scores with those before you started the pleasurable activities regimen. Pay attention to the ways in which your relationship has improved in other areas since you started having more fun together. In addition, note the drop in your stress level with the addition of both joint and independent pleasurable activities to your daily schedule.

Make Each Other Laugh

Getting a good laugh out of someone you love can be enormously rewarding. Both people reap the health benefits of laughter. Moreover, the one who is made to laugh cannot help but feel a rush of positive feelings toward the other for putting forth the effort to elicit laughter and joy. And, of course, the one who provokes the laughter feels appreciated and reinforced.

Any relationship that reverberates with laughter will be a haven from stress and a place where you will want to spend your time. This is not to say that you should laugh at anything or everything—certainly not things that are sad, tragic, or truly serious. Nor would you want a relationship based on pure laughter, with no serious or deeper dimension. Notwithstanding such unusual excesses, laughter remains the best medicine for people and their relationships.

Generally, in relatively early stages of relationships, partners periodically put forth efforts to generate laughter. They try to be entertaining, witty, or funny; they send humorous cards or notes to cheer up the other's day. But, as time goes on and relationships become more established, the efforts frequently ebb along with the laughter. Building more fun into your relationship means making the effort again to give your partner and yourself the pleasure of laughter.

The ways to generate laughter are too numerous to list and depend largely on your individual senses of humor. The efforts you make to get a laugh out of your partner don't have to be excessive or extreme. Buying a funny card, cutting out an amusing cartoon, or buying an audio or video cassette of a favorite comedian are small but generally effective gestures. Once in a while, a more extravagant attempt is warranted. You will find that the anticipation and planning will provide you with at least as much pleasure as your partner will finally experience.

Celebrate Your Efforts

Celebrations create pleasure. Now that you have committed yourselves to the process of detoxifying your relationship and living in the pleasure zone, you have something very special to celebrate together: your joint efforts to make your relationship healthy.

There is no point in waiting until everything is totally remedied before you celebrate. Periodically celebrating your efforts along the way will provide reinforcement for the important work you are doing and the ongoing process of recovery.

Once a month, on the anniversary of the day that you started making your relationship better (or as close to the date as possible), hold a celebration. Plan something festive to do together and count it as a pleasurable activity for the day. Try to do something a little different each month to keep the sense of festivity fresh.

You deserve a more elaborate celebration when you reach the six-month milestone, and an even more festive one at your one-year detoxification anniversary. Perhaps a weekend vacation is in order, or a very special night on the town. Whatever you decide, be sure you both enjoy it and remember to praise each other for your hard work.

Take the time to tell your partner what he or she has done that has been particularly meaningful to you. Let your partner know the ways in which you feel better about the relationship. In addition, use the opportunity to set some specific goals for further improvement to reach by the next monthly celebration.

In a real sense, you are celebrating the rebirth of your relationship. Together, you have rescued it from a perilous state of toxicity and saved your health in the process. Here's to both of you!

20

⚹══════⚹══════⚹

What to Do If It Can't Be Fixed

This chapter is not about failure. It is about maintaining your sense of psychological freedom—believing that you still have options to relieve your unhappiness and regain your physical and emotional health even when you lack any desire to detoxify your damaged relationship or when your attempts to do so have not been successful.

The cumulative toxic effects of negative emotions endured over a long period of time can obscure your perception that ways to improve the quality of your life still do exist. The negative feelings can create so much emotional burnout and demoralization that you may doubt your strength even to exercise the available options.

Stuck in the throes of self-doubt and perceived entrapment, you may become preoccupied with the idea that you must, at all costs, avoid "failure." The encompassing concern implies that terminating your relationship as it presently exists would be tantamount to "giving up," "being a loser," "failing," or "being a quitter."

This kind of thinking understandably paralyzes action. You have misconstrued what may well be the only way out of a bad situation to mean that you have failed or, worse, that you *are* a failure. However, alternative ways to think about your problem should help you see that there is, indeed, light at the end of your dark tunnel.

First, consider another interpretation of the term *failure*. Think of a person who fails as a person who does not even try. The biggest hitters in the history of baseball frequently struck out. Yet, they always went up to the plate and *tried* to get a hit. Of course, if they hadn't entered the game to begin with, they wouldn't have had to endure the disappointment of striking out. But they would never have known the euphoria of hitting a home run, either. The fellow who lacks the courage to walk up to the plate and give it his best shot has failed because he hasn't even tried to play the game.

If you have tried—albeit unsuccessfully—to make your relationship work, *you* haven't failed. Admittedly, you haven't experienced a complete success, but that is not the same thing as failing. The correct question to ask now is not how to avoid failure, but what to do when you determine that the relationship is a bad investment in your good health and future.

When to Cut Your Losses

Making the decision to terminate a close relationship because it has become irreparably toxic and harmful to your health can be very tough. It can also be the most important and best decision you will ever make, since your very survival may depend on it.

I cannot tell you exactly if or when to leave a toxic relationship. Ultimately, that must be your decision. I can, however, suggest ways to evaluate your situation with the benefit of my years of helping patients through these difficult choices.

There are some useful analogies to the decision you are weighing. First, think of yourself as a person who has lost money in an investment that has turned sour. At this point, you still have some assets left. The issue is whether to invest even more of your remaining money in the same deal, with the hope that somehow you'll regain your losses and even wind up a winner, or to protect whatever assets remain in order to have them available for future, possibly far more successful ventures. You want to avoid throwing good money after bad.

The years you have left to live, the quality of your life, your physical and psychological health, your time, effort, self-esteem, and energy are just some of the assets you have invested and can continue to invest in the relationship. You must decide how much of your remaining emotional funds—and other material wealth—you are willing to risk losing before letting go of the hope that your relationship will stop hurting.

Or, think of your relationship as being kept alive through some artificial means such as a relationship life-support system. Maintaining the relationship under such conditions involves enormous costs and precious few rewards. Your decision is really about whether to continue maintaining the pretense of a vital relationship despite the fact that all or almost all of your positive feelings have died, and that the painful costs of your negative emotions have become nearly or totally unbearable.

Let me remind you that we are talking about preserving the lives of the individuals involved in a relationship that is "near death." When you have tried to make changes but the results have been disappointing or negligible, the one remaining option may have to be pulling the plug on the relationship and letting *it* die so that *you* can live.

The ambivalence or guilt that your decision might evoke may have to be resolved after the fact. Once the decision is made, you then can bolster your choice by reviewing the efforts you made, the pain you felt, the endangerment to your health, and, finally, the fact that the odds were very poor that your relationship would ever recover any semblance of healthy function.

An orthopedic surgeon once pointed out to me the parallel between losing a love relationship and losing a limb. The doctor explained that when a patient is told he has a gangrenous limb

238

that must be amputated, the patient often becomes panicked about losing a part of his body.

The doctor's response under those difficult circumstances is to show the patient that in fact he already lost his limb when the infection destroyed it. Now, he is not losing an arm or a leg but getting rid of a toxic appendage that will kill the rest of him if he does not consent to amputate it. While the patient can cry for the loss of his limb, he must recognize that the loss came long before the decision to sever it.

Similarly, if your relationship is so toxic that it literally imperils your health and life, you must cut it off to save yourself. You will understandably cry over the loss of your love. But you really lost the love a while ago; now what you have is a relationship filled with negative emotions that has been unhealthy for a very long time.

Relating these parallel experiences to the decision you face will widen your perspective and help you identify some of your resistances to ending your toxic relationship. Many of my patients have found the discussions we have had using these analogies pivotal in the resolution of their relationship crises.

Of course, there are other aspects of your current situation to examine and evaluate in order to make your decision. One of the most important considerations should be the state of your physical and psychological health. Have you already become ill perhaps, in part, because of the toxic feelings your relationship has generated? Are you failing to recover because of the ongoing stress that dealing with your relationship produces? If your answers are affirmative, then you should be moved a step closer to letting go of the relationship in order to save yourself.

You may so far have managed to escape the onset of either physical or emotional illness, although you undoubtedly have many signs of being under chronic stress if you are involved in a toxic relationship. But, consider your medical history and that of your family. Have you ever had any illness or problems that have gone into remission but that you know may return under conditions of too much stress? Is there a history of heart disease, cancer, diabetes, or arthritis in your family? These are just a few of the illnesses whose causes or exacerbations are thought to be due to a physiological predisposition triggered by current life stress and an excess of negative emotions. If you know of a disease lurking in your personal or family history that could be triggered by the toxic relationship you are in, then weigh carefully the risk of staying in it, and govern yourself accordingly.

Next, take a good look at your current health habits and ways of dealing with stress. Do you drink more than you should? Do you find yourself turning to alcohol to calm down, or to boost your mood because your relationship makes you feel so low? Do you use other drugs for the same purposes or to help you blunt the pain and hurt?

Do you smoke cigarettes and find yourself too stressed, irritable, or just insufficiently motivated to stop because you are distracted by the relationship problems in your life? Have you lost control of your weight because you feel frustrated, rejected, and angry? And what about your overall level of physical fitness—is it unacceptable too?

Holding on to your toxic relationship may function as a convenient excuse to keep you from taking proper care of yourself and regaining your health. If that is the case, think again about the high price you are paying and the disaster you are courting by staying hooked in a destructive bond.

Finally, make a list of the Seven Deadly Signs of Toxic Relationships to carry around with you for five days. Each time that you experience any of the toxic feelings in response to your relationship, make a check mark on your list.

At the end of five days, sit down and look long and hard at your tallies. Imagine each mark as a small dose of psychological poison. Then, do some mental arithmetic and project your five-day experience out to a year's worth of toxic emotions. Imagine how much poison you would receive during the next five years if you stayed in the relationship. Are you still willing to continue with it?

How to Leave Your Lethal Lover

As the songwriter Paul Simon said, there must be "fifty ways to leave your lover." All of them pretty much add up to the same bottom line: Get up and get out. All else are details that can and will be worked out later.

Until you accept this fundamental reality, you will remain entangled in your dangerous, toxic relationship. In addition, the protracted pain of wanting out but not leaving will wreak the same kind of havoc on your self-esteem and health as do other kinds of self-destructive addictions.

The way for an alcoholic to save his or her life is to stop drinking. The way for a cocaine addict to break the all-consuming hold and regain his or her health is to give up the drug. The way to end your addiction to a Lethal Lover or toxic relationship is to exit.

I realize, of course, that the solution sounds easier than its implementation. Remember, I help people with these kinds of problems for a living. I know and appreciate how much courage it takes to break an addiction and/or end a relationship. But, to save yourself, you must find that courage.

Don't put off acting on your decision until you and your lover or spouse agree on the reasons your relationship must end, or on whether it should even end at all. And don't postpone, delay, or protract your exit until you and your partner have resolved every detail of the breakup. Chances are that you won't agree. You haven't seen things eye to eye during the time you've been together, so why expect things to be suddenly different now that you are coming apart?

The breakup of your toxic relationship may involve further negative emotions for a while. But that's the key: for *a while*, not indefinitely. When you decide to end your relationship and in fact leave your Lethal Lover, the relief from the negativity will be within sight. How quickly you get there depends on how committed you are to making yourself healthy again.

The extent of contact and interaction you need to have with your former spouse or lover after the termination of your relationship depends primarily on the presence of mediating factors such as joint investments, common friends, or, most important, children. If there are no reasons that make it necessary for you to have contact with your ex-partner, then the most advisable course is to break the bond completely. Missing your Lethal Lover should *not* be accepted as an excuse to reconnect. The addict who decides to get clean from heroin or cocaine cannot permit himself to use again periodically simply because he misses the drug.

When other factors are present, particularly children, it will be necessary to have contact and desirable to keep your relationship on civil terms. You will have to discuss certain decisions pertaining to your children and to arrange for visitation and other matters. Sustaining hostilities and resentments under such circumstances is harmful to both you and your children. Professional help should be sought to help neutralize the residual negative emotions, work out agreements, and develop methods for raising your children as divorced parents in a way that is best for them.

If you do not completely cut off your contact with your ex-partner, you will certainly need to redefine your relationship into a new category. Hopefully, you will be terminating the bond that was toxic and redefining it as a different and less intimate relationship that can operate without the same degree of negativity. So, for example, a divorced couple may be able to relate to each other as parents of the same children without the intimacy and negativity of their marital roles.

Similarly, some former lovers or spouses decide to redefine their relationships into friendships. Sometimes this works; more often, in my experience, the lethal connection that was damaging in the romantic bond continues to have negative effects in the context of a friendship. In any event, it is usually quite difficult to move backward from intimacy to friendship without at least some considerable interval during which you cease contact and allow each other to establish new primary-love bonds with other people.

How to Terminate Other Toxic Relationships

The termination of other kinds of relationships that are harmful to your health is constrained by whether the bond is essentially voluntary or involuntary.

Voluntary relationships are those that you have freely chosen to form and that you can therefore choose to terminate. They include, for example, friendships and dating relationships. Also included are some work relationships either where you have control over the other person's employment (e.g., he or she works for you) or where you have the flexibility to relocate work settings or quit your present job.

Involuntary relationships are primarily family ties, particularly blood connections. The latter, of course, are relationships into which you were born rather than ones you have chosen. Work relationships may also be thought of as involuntary where you have no control over the other person's employment status (e.g., you work for him or her, or you are both employees reporting to supervisors), or where you have a very low degree of flexibility and very high costs attached to leaving your place of employment.

You can and should terminate a highly toxic, voluntary relationship by severing the tie completely. There is no point in maintaining a friendship with anyone who causes you so much stress, anger, aggravation, or pain that your health is imperiled. As the old saying goes, with friends like that, you don't need enemies.

Similarly, if a voluntary work relationship has become irreversibly toxic, you will need to terminate it. When the other person's behavior has had a demonstrable negative impact on job performance or on your business, and when you are in a position to terminate that person's employment, you will need to do so to protect yourself, your business, and the morale of your other employees.

If the fellow worker is not someone over whom you exercise control but with whom the interaction has become toxic and damaging to your health and job performance, you will need to consider alternatives to your current employment. If you can readily transfer, do so; if possible, take steps to seek a mediated solution to the problem that might result in the other person's transfer, relocation, or termination.

When a work relationship is involuntary and you have very little flexibility to change jobs, you will need to take interim steps to minimize the damage of the relationship until a formal change in your present working conditions can occur. Given that your career or job is implicated, your motivation to try to detoxify the relationship should be high.

If you cannot detoxify it, you will need to establish a safer psychological distance from the person who is so stressful to you. Minimize the amount of interaction by keeping it limited exclusively to job-related conversation.

When the toxic relationship is with your employer or supervisor, and you value your position or the company for which you work, you should seek the relevant employee assistance program counseling or other professional help. In many respects, a job is like a marriage, and a toxic relationship in the workplace can be every bit as harmful to your health as a Lethal Lover can. To save your well-being, self-esteem, and long-term career goals, you may need to divorce your current employer.

Finally, there is the very difficult issue of how to handle involuntary toxic relationships that can't be fixed, specifically blood ties. Because of their complexity, when family relationships become toxic, the damage to your emotional and physical health can be extreme and life-threatening. Parent-child feuds and sibling conflicts are common examples.

There is no easy or complete solution to the toxic family relationship. You must make the choice as to whether you need to sever your relationship completely. Although such total breaks are relatively rare, they do occur. And they certainly must when a family member is truly pathological in ways that cause physical abuse, sexual abuse, or psychological violence.

Short of those extremes, toxic family relationships that cause high levels of stress, discomfort, tension, aggravation, or unhappiness are fairly commonplace. Whenever possible, attempts should be made to detoxify the relationships through improved communication, problem solving, boosting positive feelings, and, of course, professional help if possible. There are many benefits and rewards to family bonds that offset their costs.

However, to protect your health, it may be necessary to achieve a greater degree of psychological distance from your toxic relative. Psychological distance refers to less intimacy and lower interdependence. You will need to reduce the amount of information about yourself, particularly of an intimate or personal nature, that you disclose to the relative in question. If you still crave a withholding parent's approval, you must learn to rely on your own sense of self-affirmation and the feedback of other people with whom you have healthier relationships.

Disruptions in blood relationships are often far reaching due to the very nature of families. A falling-out between siblings, for example, will likely have negative consequences on parents, other siblings, and perhaps cousins, nieces and nephews, and aunts and uncles. Still, as with any other toxic relationship that can't or won't be fixed, you must decide what actions are necessary to protect yourself from a damaging family member. And, you will probably need to do some maintenance work to preserve your relationships with other family members whom you love and who are affected by or disapproving of your rift.

Surviving Relationship Stress

Few people get through life without having some difficult and damaging relationships along the way. The key to surviving relationship stress lies in detoxifying the bonds that can be changed and removing or distancing yourself from the ones that can't. No benefit is gained by merely enduring the pain and stress and suffering silently.

Withstanding inevitable life stress without succumbing to illness depends on cultivating the mentality of a survivor—and that is the subject of our final chapter.

21

◄══════◄══════◄

Creating Hardy Relationships for Life

For the first time in the eleven years of their married life, Linda and Peter both are committed to the challenge of sustaining a healthy marriage based on mutual love, respect, open communication, and fidelity.

After suffering through several months of knowing that Peter was involved in his third extramarital affair, Linda finally mustered the courage to confront her husband. Psychotherapy plus stern warnings from her doctor about the risk of developing colon cancer convinced Linda to act in order to save her physical and mental health.

At first, Peter cried, apologized, and implored her to work with him to save their marriage and recapture their love. He agreed to come to joint therapy sessions. There, he acknowledged that his acts of unfaithfulness were, in part, provoked by the unexpressed anger and resentment he had harbored for many years against Linda because, in his view, she made him feel "guilty and inadequate."

On her part, Linda dropped her attitude of righteous indignation within a few sessions of joint therapy and acknowledged her contributions to the deterioration of their marriage. At a critical juncture, Linda and Peter were asked to search their souls in order to decide whether there were enough positive feelings left in their relationship to warrant an intensive effort at detoxification.

The commitment was made to turn their marriage around. Within six weeks of the detoxification program, Linda and Peter felt encouraged. They had rediscovered many of the initial qualities about their relationship that had led them to marry in the first place. They worked hard on solving their identified problems. In many respects, Linda and Peter were an exemplary pair in their discipline and desire to repair their badly damaged relationship.

So far, they have succeeded. Their marriage is thriving on positive emotions. Most important, as their relationship has become healthier, so have Linda and Peter as individuals. Their physical health problems mostly have remitted or healed. Emotionally, both describe themselves as being in the best state they can recall since having their first child ten years ago.

Linda and Peter are survivors. They have managed to avoid the divorce wars and have worked to become trusted friends and committed lovers. Together and separately, Linda and Peter have learned to develop the traits of the hardy personality: control, commitment, and challenge. In so doing, they have created a hardy relationship that will buffer them against the inevitable stresses they will face over their lifetimes together.

Dan is in the intensive coronary-care unit of the hospital after suffering a massive heart attack. Unable to break the yoke of oppression from his lethal boss, Hank, Dan's cardiovascular system succumbed to his toxic emotions created by the dual pressure-cooker environments at work and at home. His abusive drinking and heavy cigarette smoking put him at even greater risk for the destructive cardiac event.

Dan's wife is praying for his recovery. She is also hoping that when he is better, Dan will not return to his job. She knows that Dan has to stop smoking and drinking; and that together they face the challenge of fixing a broken marriage.

Although her husband's health crisis has presented her with the greatest stress she can recall facing, she feels able to cope. Her hardy personality traits are surfacing, carrying her and the family through the crisis.

Dan's wife views the heart attack in paradoxically optimistic terms: "Maybe this was the shock Dan needed to get him out of that sick relationship with Hank," she reasons. She rallies to the challenge, committed to her husband and to his recovery. As she waits through each long hour of this critical time, she searches her mind for every way that she can help and encourage Dan. Her anxiety is quelled as she uncovers opportunities to exercise control.

Dan's survival is an open question. Although he may pull through the heart attack, his longer-term personality traits require major attention. The good news is that, if he *chooses* to live out the remainder of his life in a healthy way, a good deal of support from his family, doctors, and self-help groups is available to him.

Remember Louise and Robert, the dangerous dancers? Well, they finally got married and Louise had the baby she had so long desired. However, Louise and Robert are still dancing up a storm. Their marriage is only a variation of their rocky, addictive courtship. Just a few months after their wedding, they separated for a month and then reconciled.

Louise and Robert remain hooked on their toxic cycle of withdrawal and conflict followed by intensified intimacy and a renewed "honeymoon" period. They have yet to deal with their motives and behavior. Now husband and wife, they still remain Lethal Lovers.

Many life stresses—both positive and negative—have confronted them during the first two years of their marriage. An economic recession and Louise's extended maternity leave crealed significant financial pressure; Robert changed jobs; the baby was born; and both sets of their parents suffered serious illnesses. Instead of drawing strength from each other, Louise and Robert have each become more vulnerable individually, while their already frail bond has become further strained.

Clearly, neither Louise nor Robert has a survivor personality. When stress strikes, they each become angry and point the finger of blame at the other, while they rail futilely against fate that so many problems have affected their lives.

Louise and Robert do not understand that stress and change are inevitable parts of life that can only be successfully met with the hardy attitudes of control, commitment, and challenge. To the contrary, both regress into tailspins of helplessness and loss of control. Their marriage, as shaky as their courtship, hardly represents a commitment to values worth preserving.

Louise and Robert continue to stumble through life, *reacting* to one stressor after the next. Neither has shown an ability to rise to the challenge of meeting their problems head on, perhaps even to avert some before they happen. Nor are they hopeful that their relationship will provide the support and stability they need. Sadly, both know it will not.

Stress-Resistant Relationships

Healthy relationships function as a safe haven against the inevitable vicissitudes of life. They do so in the same way as hardy personalities protect individuals. By embodying the key elements of hardiness—control, commitment, and challenge— the healthy relationship provides psychological armor that shields the partners from the most damaging effects of life stress.

Because the internal dynamics that produce negative emotions and toxic stress in the relationship are kept to a minimum, the partners are not weakened or drained by their tie. In fact, by virtue of their healthy behavior toward each other, both partners function more effectively in many areas *outside* of their relationship. For example, partners in stress-resistant relationships are more successful in their jobs, have better friendships, and maintain more balanced, functional family relationships. They look and feel healthier and more attractive and enjoy good, solid self-esteem. Of paramount importance, their individual hardiness is so solidified that they effectively ward off illness even in the face of high stress.

In many respects, it is more demanding to create and maintain a healthy, stress-resistant relationship than to endure or wallow in the negativity of a toxic one. The latter requires only that you lapse into your basest self, allowing poisonous feelings to take over.

The effort required to build healthy relationships and to keep love alive is intensely rewarding even as it is demanding. The challenge of keeping a relationship honest, vital, loving, and strong requires that you rise to your finest self. And, because the relationship you have built allows you to express your best qualities, your commitment to it is enhanced.

Maintaining a quality love relationship also requires an ever-vigilant awareness of toxic processes in their earliest, incipient form. By recognizing negative emotions in yourself and understanding how your interaction with your partner may contribute to them, you will be in the best position to neutralize psychological poisons.

Keeping toxicity at bay means that you and your partner together establish an emotional early warning system. By scanning your relationship periodically for negative behavior or feelings, and practicing joint problem solving as soon as the threat is detected, your relationship will remain protected.

Finally, the partners of a stress-resistant relationship stand ready to bolster each other when outside stressors strike. They close ranks and face the common enemy together, rather than turning on each other, splintering their bond with anxiety and anger.

Healthy partners who survive the stress of life do so by reminding each other consistently and consciously of what each can do to increase their sense of *control* in the eye of a storm; that stress can be seen as a *challenge* that strengthens their bond because they will cope with problems together; and that, whatever happens, their mutual *commitment* is to love each other well, to value life by protecting their health, and to make each other happy.

A Final Thought

Being able to create and sustain a healthy love relationship for life rests on your capacity to *believe* that it is possible. Toxic relationships, Lethal Lovers, and negative emotional experiences undermine that belief and sometimes destroy it.

I hope that this book has given you a reason to affirm that good relationships that can withstand stress and the test of time are indeed possible and attainable—not that they can be had only by other people, but that they are possible for *you*.

I haven't tried to do this by inventing fairy tales or by withholding what must have seemed, on occasion, to be fairly brutal truths. Instead, I have introduced you to many of the real people (with details and names changed to protect confidentiality) who have enriched my professional life and taught me much of what I know. Most of them have solved their toxic relationship problems. I also have offered you many ways to help yourself make life-changing and maybe even life-saving choices.

Ultimately, your own experience will be the best teacher. My fondest and final thought is that this book will launch you on the pursuit of healthy love. I believe that when you indeed find it, you will believe in it, too.

References

Chapter Two

[1]Justice, B. *Who Gets Sick*. Los Angeles: Jeremy Tarcher Press, 1988.

[2]Kobasa, S. C. Stressful life events, personality and health: An inquiry into hardiness. *Journal of Personality and Social Psychology* 37(1), 1979, 1–11.

[3]Justice, B. *Op. cit.*

Chapter Four

[4]Williams, R. B., Jr., T. L. Haney, K. L. Lee, Y. H. Kong, J. A. Blumenthal, and R. E. Whalen. Type A behavior, hostility, and coronary atherosclerosis. *Psychosomatic Medicine* 42(6), 1980, 539–49.

[5]LeShan, L., and R. E. Worthington. Personality as a factor in the pathogenesis of cancer: A review of the literature. *British Journal of Medical Psychology* 29, 1956, 49–56.

Chapter Eight

[6]Bahnson, C. B. The patient with cancer. In Sutnick, A. (ed.), *Oncologic Medicine*. University Park: University Park Press, 1976.

[7]Solomon, G. F., L. Temoshok, A. O'Leary, and J. Zich. An intensive psychoimmunologic study of long-surviving persons with AIDS. *Annals of the New York Academy of Science* 486, 1987, 647–55.

[8]Siegel, B. *Peace, Love and Healing*. New York: Harper & Row, 1989.

[9]*Ibid.*

[10]*Psychology Today*, September 1989, 24.

REFERENCES

[11]Julius, M., E. Harburg, and E. Cottington. Marital pair anger-coping types and all-cause mortality in Tecumseh (1971–1983 Follow Up). Paper presented at the 39th Annual Scientific Meeting of Oncological Society of America, Chicago, November 19–23, 1986.

Chapter Eleven

[12]Seligman, M. *Helplessness: On Depression, Development and Death.* San Francisco: Freeman, 1975.

[13]Maier, S. F., and M. Seligman. Learned helplessness: Theory and evidence. *Journal of Experimental Psychology: General* 105, 1976, 3–46.

[14]Seligman, M. *Learned Optimism.* New York: Knopf, 1991.

[15]Siegel, B. *Op. cit.*

[16]———. *Love, Medicine and Miracles.* New York: Harper & Row, 1988.

Chapter Twelve

[17]Siegel, B. *Peace, Love and Healing.* New York: Harper & Row, 1989.

[18]*Ibid.*

[19]Harlow, H. F. The nature of love. *American Psychologist* 13, 1958, 673–85.

Chapter Thirteen

[20]Selye, H. Personal interview. *Psychology Today* 11(10), March 1978, 60–70.

[21]American Psychiatric Association. *Diagnostic and Statistical Manual of Mental Disorders*, 3rd edition, revised. Washington, D.C.: American Psychiatric Association, 1987.

Chapter Fourteen

[22]Selye, H. *Op. cit.*